Garcia, Enrique,
1975- author.

The Hernandez
brothers

DISCARD

D1737943

the
hernande

love, rockets, and

LATINO AND LATIN AMERICAN PROFILES
Frederick Luis Aldama, Editor

z brothers

alternative comics

ENRIQUE GARCÍA

UNIVERSITY OF PITTSBURGH PRESS

Published by the University of Pittsburgh Press, Pittsburgh, Pa., 15260

Cataloging-in-Publication data is available from the Library of Congress

ISBN 13: 978-0-8229-6492-6
ISBN 10: 0-8229-6492-9

Cover illustration courtesy of Fantagraphics Books, Inc.,
used with permission of the artists
Cover design by Joel W. Coggins

To Nikolina Dobreva,
my support and inspiration.

contents

preface

My *Poison River* Fiasco

THE FIRST TIME I read any work by Gilbert or Jaime Hernandez, I was completing my PhD in comparative literature at the University of Massachusetts Amherst in 1999. I was taking a graduate survey class on twentieth-century Spanish American fiction that included canonical pieces by Gabriel García Márquez, Julio Cortázar, and other greats. My professor had chosen Tomás Rivera's novel *...y no se lo tragó la tierra* and Gilbert Hernandez's graphic novel *Poison River* to represent Mexican American/Chicano/Latino narratives. At the beginning of the semester, all the students in the class had to choose a book to discuss and present in class, and I selected *Poison River* because I have always been an avid comic book reader, fan, and collector and was excited to be able to discuss graphic fiction at an advanced graduate level.

After I bought my copy of *Poison River* at the beginning of the semester, I began to read it out of curiosity but could not stop until I finished the entire text several hours later. I was astonished by the book because of the quality of Gilbert Hernandez's art, the complexity of his narrative, the subversive nature of the text, and the epic ambition that only a few master comic creators like Alan Moore or Osamu Tezuka could achieve. I think discovering *Poison River* redeemed my faith in comics, but also in academia because my

Luba witnesses Ofelia's rape. Gilbert Hernandez, *Beyond Palomar*, 46. © Gilbert Hernandez.

professor, Luis Marentes, was brave enough to place a Latino graphic novel in his canonical survey.

As I was preparing for my presentation, I found out that what I was reading in *Poison River* was not a graphic novel with original content, but mostly a reprinting (with some additional new pages) of a storyline that had previously appeared in the Hernandez brothers' alternative comic anthology *Love and Rockets*. Before my presentation, I went to the alternative music stores in Amherst to buy more of Los Bros Hernandez's previous work because I wanted to know more about their visual style and how it developed through the years. As I began to figure out the complexity of Gilbert's Palomar stories, I thought it was too much material for my presentation and decided to introduce just some basic elements of the *Love and Rockets* anthology and keep most of my discussion limited to *Poison River*, the text assigned for class discussion.

The day of my presentation finally arrived. Very enthusiastic, I provided visual examples of Gilbert Hernandez's art, explained the visual and narrative devices he used to tell his story, and talked about how these differed from the narrative tools used by the other prose writers we had discussed in class. When the discussion was opened to the other students, I was taken aback by the outrage many of them expressed about the book. A number of the graduate students hailed from Spain and countries in Latin America and were very angry because they were offended by the violence (specifically Ofelia's rape) in *Poison River*.[1] They also thought the narrative was misogynist because of Gilbert Hernandez's visual portrayal of Luba's enormous breasts.

The professor acknowledged that readers could be offended by the violence and sex included in the book but counter-argued that similar erotic and violent scenes had also appeared in the canonical literature we had previously studied in class. He proposed that the issues the students had with the book were related to the fact that it was a visual medium, yet many did not change their opinion.[2]

One of the problems I noticed in the discussion was that most of the graduate students were not familiar with comic book narratives, the intricacies of their language, and the difference between funny strips for children and graphic novels for adults. The whole class had been designed to teach and appreciate narratives written in prose, and suddenly "this *Poison River* text" had a different method of narration, abounded in intertextual references, and was infused with American/Latino/Chicano sensibilities that functioned similarly to—yet differently from—the canonical storytelling promoted in traditional Hispanic nation-states. I believe that most of the students reacted badly to the abrupt shift in narrative from an aesthetic, formalistic, and ethnic point of view, which made me realize that I needed to incorporate a different approach when teaching Los Bros Hernandez's work in my own classes.

Interestingly, Gilbert Hernandez satirized the existing widespread ignorance about comics in the segment "Venus Tells It Like It Is."[3] In this one-page strip, the author's acclaimed comic character Luba hears that her young grandniece Venus reads mostly comics. She reacts in a positive manner to the news because, as revealed in the *Poison River* storyline, she herself learned to read with comic books. She asks if they still make them today, both showing her ignorance about the current state of the industry and her association of the medium with her childhood. Luba thus represents a large group of potential readers who may have nostalgic notions about the juvenile comic narratives they read in childhood but who do not have any idea about adult comic book narratives because they did not continue reading comics as they matured and grew older. At the end of the strip, Venus's mother remarks that "although most of them are very bad, the best ones are as compelling and enriching as any other art form."[4] With this statement, Hernandez admits the existence of many mediocre comics that inundate the market while damaging the medium's prestige but affirms his belief in the potential of a medium that has often been associated solely with children's fantasies.

When I was asked to contribute an entry to the Contemporary Latino Writers and Directors series, I jumped at the opportunity to write an introductory book to Los Bros' comic book masterpieces. My main goal is to write a book that is accessible enough to entice non-comic readers interested in finding out more about the Hernandez brothers' work while providing compelling discussion points to fans who have read all their work several times and who know every single detail about their characters. It is very important to note here that, although I am a fan of Gilbert and Jaime Hernandez's work, I will address their most criticized aspects (exploitative and sexualized storytelling) in addition to what are generally perceived as their strengths (artistic values, narrative ambition, original ethnic and gender representations).

acknowledgments

FIRST AND FOREMOST, I want to thank the Hernandez Brothers for their amazing body of work, and to Gilbert and Jaime in particular for granting me the personal interview that gave center and direction to this book. My sincerest gratitude goes to Frederick Aldama for starting this series and supporting me throughout the project. I am also very indebted to him as a model in work and life. Your energy, commitment, and inspiring research have always kept me going. ¡Gracias, mano! Another formative influence who has had a direct bearing on this book has been my professor and friend Luis Marentes. Your classes, your comments on my graduate projects, as well as our endless discussions then and now on anything from arts to world politics, have been instrumental to my development as a scholar, as have been your transnational approach to Latin American studies and your openness to nonstandard topics. Most importantly, I first encountered and fell in love with the work of Los Bros Hernandez in one of your classes.

The Hernandez Brothers

LOVE, ROCKETS, AND ALTERNATIVE COMICS

introduction

LOS BROS HERNANDEZ are a collective of sibling Latino comic book artists (Mario, Gilbert, and Jaime) who have been very influential in the American comic book industry. Born to a humble Mexican-American family in Oxnard, California, the brothers have taken an interesting career path to develop into the artists they are today. Their seminal experimental anthology *Love and Rockets* is their most important achievement, as it is one of the longest-running titles that has survived on the ever-changing comic book market, and is the text that fully demonstrates their artistic maturity. With this work, they have been able to experiment with comic book narrative techniques, which has earned them a loyal fan base and the respect of their peers in the industry as well as that of mainstream critics.

Gilbert and Jaime Hernandez, the main subjects of this book, are arguably two of the most influential U.S. Latino comic book artists of all time. They self-identify specifically as Latino artists (of Mexican American descent), and their collective work includes masterpieces such as Gilbert's *Palomar* and Jaime's *Locas* sagas. Their epic stories contain Latino characters and content that often serve to define their texts as ethnic contributions to the American comic book industry, which has been known for having a problematic history in providing venues for diversity. However, not all of their comics feature Latino signifiers, and, as Los Bros are very comfortable with mainstream American comic book genres, they are able to dabble in narratives that in the past were not commonly associated with traditional Latino literature, such as superheroes, horror, and science fiction.

Both brothers have been able to create successful stories enjoyed by all types of audiences, yet have still firmly established their identity as alternative Latino creators. Their works have been critically acclaimed by scholars who regularly write essays about their work, while their sales figures have kept them in print over several decades, and they have become two of the more recognizable names of the prominent independent comic book company Fantagraphics Books. They have also published additional material in mainstream publishing giants such as DC Comics, the *New York Times*, and the *New Yorker*. The controversial nature of their comic book content, specifically in terms of sex and violence, does not always allow them to profit from the teen market that tends to dominate the American comic book industry, but it certainly has made them iconic in alternative and intellectual circles.

As a fan of comic books and graphic novels, and as a Puerto Rican/Hispanic/Latino reader, I've had a difficult time narrowing down the traits that define a great Latino artist. The American comic book industry has had important contributions from a number of Latino comic book writers/artists, such as George Pérez (Puerto Rican heritage) and Joe Quesada (Cuban heritage), who have helped to develop the visual aesthetics and storytelling of mainstream superhero narratives (for example, in their work on the Avengers/New Teen Titans and the Batman/Daredevil series, respectively). Their comics tend to be family friendly and directed to a mainstream audience, and, even though the creators are of Hispanic descent, their work does not provide too many Latino signifiers that might confuse its target mainstream audience.[1] There are dozens of creators of Latino/Hispanic descent working in the American comic book industry, and many have created important pieces that are aesthetically impressive. However, the vast majority of their work is limited to the genres and topics promoted by the mainstream American comic book publishing corporations. This is why the influence of Latino/Hispanic artists in the comics published in the United States tends to be very underrated.

In his book *Your Brain on Latino Comics*, scholar Frederick Aldama provides a comprehensive coverage of the history of Latino comics (with Latino subjects) that includes a wide variety of works, such as the controversially "ethnic" funny strips by Gus Arriola in the 1950s, hipster narratives such as Gil Morales's *Dupie*, mainstream and independent Latino superheroes such as Diablo and El gato negro, and the works of alternative creators such as Gilbert and Jaime Hernandez (emphasized throughout most of the book).[2] Besides the artists of Mexican American origin, Aldama also includes artists from all Latino denominations, such as Puerto Rican (David Álvarez) and Cuban (Frank Espinosa).[3] In Aldama's view, the different types of Latino representation in the American comic book industry are important in different ways because creators of Latino comics have different goals, and while some may want to convey political messages or narratives close to the ethnic experience of the community, others may just want to entertain or portray some aspects of American life in general. Latino artists are thus a broad and varied group, whose work cannot be homogenized into a specific type of storytelling or artistic expression. Aldama explains: "When studying Latino comics, we must keep centrally in mind the dimension of the author and the reader. Not by looking to biographies or interviews for those nuggets that point to a one-to-one correspondence between fiction and biographical fact, but by noting how certain visual and verbal techniques move authors (as readers) cognitively and emotionally."[4]

I personally believe that Gilbert and Jaime Hernandez are two of the greatest Latino creators in the U.S. because, as ethnic auteurs, they have been able to create narratives that subvert hegemony without falling into the didactic tendencies of many writers. More importantly, they have been able to avoid the "ghettofication" of their subjects and to create a complex intertextuality that could only be completely understood by a reader who can decode both Latino references and the visual narratives of the Anglophone American industry. The Latino/Hispanic reader may not understand everything in their narratives if he/she does not know enough about the American comic book industry to truly grasp their subversion of genres. On the other hand, there are many details that traditional comic readers may miss if they are not familiar with the influences of the Latino heritage and the entire spectrum of the American comic book industry in their work.

When I was researching material for this book, I noticed that Los Bros Hernandez have a solid presence in the American media, despite their comics almost never making the top 100 comic list in sales. They are a hit with alternative venues such as comic book and indie record stores, but are also featured in mainstream venues such as *Time*, the *New Yorker*, and the *New York Times*, where they have given interviews and published new material. Both brothers have inspired praise by contemporary prominent writers such as Junot Díaz, Alan Moore, and Neil Gaiman, who are among the most recognized authors in the literary Anglophone world. Pulitzer Prize winner Junot

Diaz, while discussing Jaime Hernandez's illustrations of his work, recognized Los Bros' comics as an inspiration for his own pursuit of a writing career and for books such as *The Brief Wondrous Life of Oscar Wao*.[5] In another interview conducted by Michael Silverblatt in the radio show *Bookworm*, he also stated that American writers in Hollywood and mainstream literature are barely catching up to *Love and Rockets* and its representation of new gender values.

Alan Moore, writer of comic masterpieces such as *Watchmen* and *Promethea*, whom I would call the Shakespeare of English-language comics, has also written to praise Jaime's work.[6] Neil Gaiman, winner of the prestigious Hugo and Nebula awards, conducted an interview with the brothers in the *Comic Journal* (reprinted in the *Love and Rockets Companion*), and chose material from Mario and Gilbert's *Citizen Rex* to be included in his collection *The Best American Comics 2010*. This is high praise indeed, and it is not limited to writers and comic book artists. Jaime and Gilbert's work has been the focus of a number of academic studies, inspiring more scholarly criticism than most other artists in the American comic industry. Many academics (such as Frederick Aldama, Charles Hatfield, and Derek Parker Royal) are interested in Los Bros' work because of their redefinition of the comic book language and their innovative approach to Latino identity and gender values, themes that are very important and debated in American academia. Gilbert and Jaime's work remains of critical interest, as the serial nature of their output keeps them continuously innovative, unlike the work of other artists whose narratives often become outdated with the passage of time.

There is ample scholarly research on the Hernandez brothers, and it is important to review it here and outline some of the general analytical trends developed in the academic criticism of their work. One of the most relevant critical studies is Frederick Aldama's book *Your Brain on Latino Comics: From Gus Arriola to Los Bros Hernandez,* which provides a compelling account of the work of a number of Latino comic artists in the United States and explains how their visual depiction of American Latinos' realities has evolved through the years. Aldama discusses the work of Gilbert and Jaime Hernandez in the context of the history of Latino narratives. Another important work is scholar Charles Hatfield's book *Alternative Comics*, which places the brothers' work in the context of the American alternative industry and explains how *Poison River* defies the conventions of the hegemonic comic book genres, while providing an in-depth analysis of its complex narrative structure.

In addition to these important manuscripts, a number of article-length scholarly publications have appeared in academic journals. Approaches and texts discussed vary widely, and the articles address topics as diverse as race representation, sexuality, spatiality, remediation, and others (such as Christopher González's and Daerick Scott's articles). An important contribution to note is the recent (summer 2013) special issue of *ImageTexT: Interdisciplinary Comic Studies* journal titled "The Worlds of the Hernandez Brothers," edited by Derek Parker Royal and Christopher González. The articles it contains, including the excellent introduction, provide a good sample of the types of scholarly criticism available. In addition, this special issue includes a bibliography of both primary and secondary sources that would be a good reference source for those who wish to undertake further studies on Los Bros.

At this point, most of the books written about Los Bros Hernandez are published by Fantagraphics Books, the company that also publishes most of the comics included in the *Love and Rockets* series. In 2013, Fantagraphics published additional books commemorating the anniversary of *Love and Rockets*, which include *Love and Rockets: The Covers* (a collection of Los Bros covers), and *Love and Rockets Companion: 30 Years (and Counting)*, a collection of some of their more detailed interviews. One important book about Los Bros not published by Fantagraphics is *The Art of Jaime Hernandez*. It focuses on Jaime in its meticulous presentation of the creator's life and work, but also contains a lot of details on Gilbert. This particular book is very engaging because writer Todd Hignite had access to the family and was able to provide a detailed account of the brothers' childhood, comic influences, and development as artists. Because of the existence of this excellent book, I will not focus on the biographical aspects of the brothers' lives, but will refer to some of these aspects whenever relevant to the themes I am exploring.

The analysis I offer in my book aims to examine the role of Los Bros in the comic book industry, the academic canon, and the Latino arts in the United States, while covering some theoretical subjects that will appeal to an academic audience, for example, aesthetic and cultural intertextuality, developments in the perception of depictions of race and ethnicity, and more abstract ideas about the role of sex in the challenging of authority and hegemony. The themes presented in this book's chapters overlap, thus the chapters work in clusters more so than as distinct units. Each chapter is followed by a "Spotlight" section, which offers a brief discussion of an important comic not mentioned earlier but touching on themes relevant to the preceding chapter. After this introduction, the first chapter, titled "Subverting the Intertextual Comic Book Corporate Structure," follows the theoretical framework developed by Mikhail Bakhtin and later Linda Hutcheon to argue that the parodies presented in *Love and Rockets* follow the legacy of Harvey Kurtzman and Robert Crumb. Further, in the first chapter I explore the evolution of Los Bros' narrative technique and how it changed from the work of fan-artists mimicking ironically the superheroes and science fiction they read as kids to the output of alternative creators whose parodic narratives redefined American comics aesthetics by making us rethink the visual language of comic books that had been stunted in the United States by the Comics Code Authority and the marketplace.

My main goal in the first chapter is to show that, as creators, the Hernandez brothers manipulate many of the genres prevalent in American popular culture, so in order to understand their work, the reader also has to understand the intricacies of the American comic book genres the artists are redefining through their parodies. In addition to studying the intertextual elements present in the *Love and Rockets* anthology, and particularly in Los Bros' first stories "Mechan-x" and "BEM," I specifically study the parody of superhero conventions in Jaime's *Locas* saga as embodied in the character of Penny Century.

The second chapter, "The Revision of Latino Experience through Comic Book Genres and Soap Opera Devices in Gilbert Hernandez's *Palomar* and Jaime Hernandez's *Locas* Sagas," explores Los Bros' position in the Latino/Chicano canon. Prominent U.S. Latino authors have worked hard to establish the presence of Americans of Hispanic heritage in mainstream U.S. literature. Some of these authors recreate the experience of the hardships that immigrant workers endure in the United States (for example, Tomás Rivera, *. . . y no se lo tragó la tierra*); others explore the complexities of their bilingual heritage (for example, Sandra Cisneros, *House on Mango Street*); still others express ambivalence toward the cultural markers that define them as Latinos (for example, Richard Rodriguez). Grounding my argument in Latino scholarship, I specifically track how empowering and problematic the commodification of Latino identity has been, a controversy that affects how we perceive Gilbert and Jaime, due to ethnic and geographical differences that can affect the national and transnational experience of the Latino individual.

The Hernandez brothers occupy a unique position among Latino writers, not only because they work in a visual medium, but also because of the way they write their characters and storylines. Their stories and featured characters are published in serial format over several decades and evolve as perceptions of Latino identity change, which helps them to remain up to date with current representational models. For the most part, their comics have overcome the nostalgia for the creation of identity that was so important in the

1960s, and their Latino characters are not necessarily always virtuous but are often prejudiced toward other ethnic or social groups. They feel comfortable with their Hispanic heritage and function well within the cultural markers of both Latin America and the United States. Bilingualism is not an issue for them. Neither is citizenship or national belonging.

In this second chapter, I focus on Gilbert's *Palomar* saga, a text particularly important for being set in both an ambiguous Latin America and the United States. As first-generation immigrants, the *Palomar* characters experience different lifestyles and attitudes, but their stories do not involve the long-distance nationalism that often permeates this type of narrative. More importantly, their progeny, second- and third-generation immigrants, who know nothing about their parents' and grandparents' past or their experiences prior to their arrival in the United States, cannot understand them or their actions. Thus, a gap opens between first-generation and second- and third-generation immigrants due to inadequate communication and the absence of shared experiences. An example of this is the *Poison River* storyline that discloses the violent origin of the character of Luba in Latin America and juxtaposes it to the extravagant lifestyle of her offspring in the United States.

I further argue that the politics of Gilbert do not always fit Latin American dialectics, as his social conflicts lack the historical references that define nationalist narratives. His criticism is mostly about the Palomar citizens that serve as a metaphor for the ostracized Latino/Chicano communities of his youth, and about how they handle the neurotic elements of sexuality. The saga also presents their journey from isolation to an age where they are finally able to represent themselves to the global world as conveyed by Fritz's movies. This idea glorifies the role of Latino/Chicano comics in opening the narrative of mass culture in order to finally communicate a specific Latino/Hispanic experience in the United States.

In the second chapter, I also cover certain aspects of Jaime Hernandez's *Locas* saga that are relevant to this discussion. I argue that Jaime's narrative was always more accessible to Anglophone audiences because it dabbles in more mainstream genres such as science fiction, punk narratives, urban melodrama, and others. Still, I focus in particular on Maggie's relationship with Rena Titañón, who represents the political side of Latino culture that is sometimes baffling to Maggie, a Latina who is not connected to a specific Latin American nation-state. The evolution of their relationship and the parallels with Penny Century's superhero obsessions that I discuss in the first chapter provide a dialogical clash of voices related to Latino identity that makes the characters feel more rounded. Rena and Penny are two models (resistance and assimilation) that Maggie respects and avoids while following her dreams of finding true happiness.

The final chapter consists of an interview I conducted with Gilbert and Jaime Hernandez when they were honored at Ohio State University as guest speakers for the Billy Ireland Cartoon Library and Museum's Grand Opening Festival of Cartoon Art in November 2013. This interview was important for the manuscript because I was able to ask them about several topics I discuss in the book and see how they responded to some of the controversial aspects related to representations of sexual relations and ethnicity that have been addressed in previous academic scholarship. This was one of the most important moments in my career, as I was able to interact with artists I truly respect, and it is a suitable conclusion for the book.

My main goal in writing this book is to provide an introductory text that allows students at the university level to understand the basic cultural elements (industry, cultural connections, ethnic and gender issues) that are truly important for the full appreciation of Los Bros Hernandez's comic books and graphic novels. Within the limits of this manuscript, I may not be able to cover every single aspect of Los Bros' prolific work or redeem the more controversial aspects of their storytelling, yet I hope my readers will be able to understand why Gilbert and Jaime are so important for Latino arts, the American comic book industry, and for American culture in general.

The American Comic Book Industry, the Comics Code, and the Control and Manipulation of Distribution Spaces

As an introduction to neophyte comic readers who have not read very many comics since they were children, I will now attempt to place Los Bros Hernandez's work within the history of the American comic book industry. Further, I will explain how certain historical events led to economic censorship related to constrictions on the physical space of distribution in the United States, which in turn led to the dominance of the superhero genre that set the industry back in terms of artistic freedom and content. I will also trace Los Bros Hernandez's work back to its origins within an alternative movement that had roots in the 1960s underground comix collective whose artists tried to reinvent the corporate language of comics and create more radical and adult projects. I will further explain how *Love and Rockets* took advantage of the new direct-market distribution system set in place in the late 1970s and early 1980s, and how its brand has evolved under the publisher Fantagraphics Books, from an outsider comic anthology marketed to more alternative readers and stores to a commercially viable product that will take advantage of the current digital distribution that may change the ways in which comics are distributed.

The availability and features of a physical retail space for the distribution of comics have been important in the history of the American comic book industry because physical space was the key to establishing economic censorship during the mid-twentieth century in a country that by law embraces a broad definition of freedom of speech. American comic book scholars (for example, Bradford Wright in *Comic Book Nation*, Bart Beaty in *Fredric Wertham and the Critique of Mass Culture*, and Amy Kiste Nyberg in *Seal of Approval: The History of the Comics Code*) have highlighted two particular historical events that helped to create the retail limitations that forever marked comic book culture in the United States: the publication of *Seduction of the Innocent* by psychiatrist Frederick Wertham in 1954, and the establishment of the Comics Code Authority, a self-censorship group created by comic book publishers (and not the American government). Wertham's book and the Comics Code are much maligned in American comic book culture today because they are blamed for the events that led to the infantilization and conservative nature of the medium on the American market. However, these were very complex historical events, where opposition to comic books came both from intellectuals and educators who needed to defend canonical literature from the waning interests of children and from religious groups who had issues about the morality of many of the exploitative comics that were printed at the time.[7]

Wertham's book helped to create a lot of debate in post–World War II United States about the role of mass culture in the upbringing of the American youth.[8] The author specifically targeted comics because he saw them in his studies as one of the main causes of illiteracy in children that could in turn lead them to a life in crime and, therefore, to poverty.[9] Scholar Bart Beaty states that the importance of Wertham's book is that "if it consolidated the anti-comic book sentiment in professional journals where it had been previously mixed, it also solidified opposition in religious magazines that had always been skeptical."[10]

Many individuals opposed Wertham's research, yet many others were inspired to galvanize a movement against the comic book industry and to pressure American senators to provide legislation that could regulate the controversial content that was published in comics at the time. Scholar Amy Kiste Nyberg writes that, as a response to public pressure, some comic book companies hastily created the Comics Code Authority, whose seal-of-approval stamp would guarantee the stores that the comics they sold had wholesome

Luba's reaction to Frida Kahlo's art. Gilbert Hernandez, *Beyond Palomar*, 37. © Gilbert Hernandez.

content.[11] The companies would therefore avoid further inquiries from the United States Senate. However, establishing the Code became a type of censorship in itself, when most newsstands stopped carrying the comics that were not officially approved by the Comics Code's office. For example, Nyberg writes that some wholesalers returned entire boxes of comics unopened because they were not carrying the Code's seal of approval.[12] This in turn led to the financial death of many companies such as EC Comics, whose comics contained more disturbing material and whose stories did not fit the Code's parameters.[13]

The Code's rules permitted depictions only of a utopian version of life. Among the most important facets of culture that were covered were regulations about the depiction of crime, specifically targeting positive portrayals of criminals and criticisms of law enforcement.[14] In addition, many bans were put in place against horror subject matter[15] (possibly targeting EC Comics and its horror line), as well as against nudity, sex, illicit marriages, divorces, and any type of behavior that defied national morality. According to Nyberg, the biggest impact the Code had on American comics was that it maintained the dominance of the superhero genre in the following years.[16] However, she finds more damaging the fact that criticism against the establishment was prohibited and therefore "without the freedom to challenge the status quo, comic book content remained for the most part quite innocuous."[17]

To contextualize what happened in the American industry in the 1950s, I wanted to compare it with similar events that happened in Mexico. Scholar

Introduction

Anne Rubinstein explains how in postrevolutionary Mexican society, comic books were similarly criticized both by educators for not being sufficiently literary and for being a threat to the postrevolutionary education of the masses, and by religious groups for providing controversial narratives. Mexico established a censor board during the 1940s, but the board's criticisms and fines were habitually ignored by the government. Comic books did not lose their space on the newsstand because the printers that published and distributed the comics were owned by politically influential newspapers with powerful political allies that allowed them to ignore the prescribed draconian punishments.[18] In addition, the laws were established to inflict penalties after distribution, not to regulate content during the creative process.[19] As a consequence, the censorship board had less power to limit the content of comic books because it could not control the space of distribution like the Code could in the United States. Nevertheless, most Mexican comics were not necessarily transgressive (with the exception of Rius's *Los supermachos* and Gabriel Vargas's *La familia Burrón* within certain specific subjects). This example is not to idealize the Mexican comic book industry, which certainly has its problems and different issues with censorship. My purpose is to compare the two types of censorship in order to demonstrate why retail space was so important in the case of the American industry. Having the Code's seal of approval would grant the comic book companies access to the American distribution system and therefore provide a more effective manner of censorship.

One interesting example provided by Rubinstein about the American conceptualization of comics as a negative influence on the working class was the work of American sociologist Oscar Lewis, who (similarly to Wertham) blamed comic book reading, alongside radio and TV, for the apathy and poverty of a second-generation-immigrant Mexican family. The family that had moved from the Mexican countryside to the capital was the focus of his study *Los hijos de Sánchez* (1961), in which Lewis also attributed one of the family's daughter's promiscuous behavior to her fascination with *Tarzan* comics in her early tomboy childhood.[20] In his *Poison River* storyline, Gilbert Hernandez addressed and parodied such intellectuals' hatred for comics in Latin American culture. In that storyline, a young Luba was constantly harassed by Ofelia and other Marxist Hispanic intellectuals who wanted her to stop reading *Pedro Pacotilla* comics (a parody of the Mexican comic *Memín Pinguín*) and to look more at Frida Kahlo paintings instead. Only her working-class father defended Luba from Ofelia's harassment, especially when Kahlo's art would make his daughter cry.[21]

Rubenstein's statement about Lewis's perception of the decay of Mexican working-class children through their consumption of mass culture is very relevant to my study of Los Bros Hernandez. In *The Art of Jaime Hernandez*, Todd Hignite explains how Los Bros' parents were workers (their father, Santos, from Mexico, and their mother, Aurora, from El Paso, Texas) who met while working in the fields and packing houses.[22] Santos died when the three brothers were still very young, which means they were mostly raised by their mother in Oxnard, California.[23] Aurora loved reading comic books, which in Mexican/Mexican American culture were also consumed by working-class adults, and she encouraged this passion in her kids.[24] The maternal support for their comic book passions allowed Mario, Gilbert, and Jaime to experience reading all types of entertainment and genres, from superheroes to jungle adventures, to funny strips and parodies. They also consumed other types of mass culture such as films and television shows which, instead of making them unfocused as Wertham or Lewis would imply, made their art visually compelling and intertextual.

Alternative Space and the Rise of *Love and Rockets*

Los Bros' parodies of the average intellectual's snobbish attitudes toward comics does not mean they support the comic book industry's hegemonic narratives. Rather, they believe in the medium and were part of the alternative movement that tried to innovate an industry stunted by the Comics Code. This would not have been possible without the underground comix movement from the 1960s and '70s that sought to break all comic taboos, or without the rise of the direct market that loosened the hold of the Comics Code.

During most of the 1960s, the Code and the limited newsstand distribution space it controlled remained mostly unchallenged. However, this began to change with the emergence of the underground scene and the hippie subculture. In the late '60s, some artists such as Robert Crumb, Spain Rodriguez, and others tried to defy the corporate and hegemonic language of the industry with their "comix" narratives that parodied or deconstructed mainstream narratives by infusing comic book art with everything that institutions like the Comics Code would not approve, such as sex, violence, and criticism of authority figures and the establishment.[25] Their use of intertextual comic images to break all taboos is very important for any discussion of Los Bros' work and will be explored in more detail in the next chapter of this book. Artistic and economic independence was the main motto of comix artists, and it allowed them to make exciting narratives without being exploited by corporations, yet it also carried some negative consequences, for example, erratic scheduling and poor profit models.

Comic book art historian Roger Sabin explains several important aspects of this underground comic book movement. First, its epicenter was in San Francisco, unlike the mainstream comic book industry's hegemony, which was based in New York City.[26] This is important to point out, especially since Los Bros are part of the California comic scene and not part of the New York publishing industry, where corporate giants like Marvel and DC Comics are located. Second, it was a movement that lasted from 1968 to 1975 and comprised mostly of self-published work, with which the Hernandez brothers were familiar.[27] Third, the artists in the movement did not have access to the newsstands because of the highly violent, erotic, and disturbing content of their works but found other ways to distribute their material, including selling their comics on the streets or in metropolitan stores that catered to customers from the alternative scene.[28]

In his book *Alternative Comics*, scholar Charles Hatfield devotes a section to the comix underground movement's influence on contemporary alternative comic artists such as Gilbert and Jaime Hernandez.[29] Among the most important contributions, Hatfield lists the fact that "comix did pave the way for a radical reassessment of the relationships among publishers, creators, and intellectual properties, a reassessment that was to affect even mainstream comics in later years. Comix were the first movement of what came to be known among fans as 'creator-owned' comic books—and creator ownership was prerequisite to the rise of alternative comics."[30] Hatfield adds that "comix introduced an 'alternative' ethos that valued the productions of the lone cartoonist over collaborative or assembly-line work. In essence, comix made comic books safe for auteur theory: they established a poetic ethos of individual expression."[31]

In the 1970s, the U.S. comic book industry began to change with the emerging direct market involving specialized comic book stores, which allowed emerging alternative comics to achieve something that the underground comix could not: national distribution. In the traditional newsstand model, distribution companies usually sent their comics to the stores, and then after a certain period, the retailers would rip off the covers of the unsold copies and send them back to the publisher. This system was not ideal because comic book companies could lose some money with the unsold copies, whereas there was no risk involved for the vendor. With the new comic book stores, owners could not return the comics they ordered, but the comic book companies would give them a larger profit margin. Even though superheroes would still be the main genre available on their stands, these owners did not use the Comics Code as a way of filtering what was supposed to be "correct" entertainment. Instead, because they needed a steady influx of customers, they attempted to comply with their buyers' interests, which, depending on the geographical location of the store or the interests of the owner, meant more available distribution space for comic book creators with alternative goals outside of the main publishing industry.[32]

To make this clearer, I will explain the pros and cons of the process of buying comics at a direct market comic book store. First, in traditional newsstands, the customer could only choose from what the retailer had exhibited. Customers did not have any power over the material being made available to them. In contrast, the new direct market established in the late 1970s allowed readers to start subscriptions through which they would individually (pre-) order material in which they were interested and would pick up on a weekly basis. Comic book stores have a large catalog where one can read the descriptions of all the material to be published in two months' time. If the reader has not missed the deadline, he/she can order whatever he/she wants from the catalog, be it *Batman* comics, Japanese manga, or other types of narratives. This system was beneficial to large and small publishers alike, as they would have a better idea of the number of titles they had to print for an established readership. In addition, they could tap into developing trends in readership, which allowed companies to experiment a little more with material that did not fit the Comics Code.

Despite these advantages to readers and publishers, the direct market can also be conservative in its own manner, as many comic book stores carry predominantly superhero and fantasy comics because they do not want to risk losing money. As Charles Hatfield explains, "This situation, only belatedly recognized as a major disadvantage, tends to discourage risk-taking by retailers, even as the economic advantages for publishers encourage the production of a surfeit of new product. The result is an excess of comic books each month, shrilly marketed, of which most retailers can order only a small sample."[33]

Before the existence of the Internet, when I was living in Puerto Rico, most of the comic stores I frequented sold almost exclusively mainstream superhero comics, which is why I did not know about Gilbert and Jaime Hernandez's work when I was growing up. I could have ordered a copy of their work if I knew about them or had browsed some of their comics in the store, but without sampling an issue of *Love and Rockets*, it would be difficult for a reader to commit to their work. This absence of information or availability of comics for instant purchase is part of a vicious circle of supply and demand disconnect, for, if there was no market for a different type of comic in my small-town store, the store owner was not going to risk losing money and order copies just so that customers can glance at the art. Thus in order for Los Bros' work to flourish in the direct market in the 1980s, there had to be alternative clients that consumed their type of storytelling that would guarantee the owner that they would come back and financially support the subscription by buying the comics they ordered.

Professor Matthew Pustz explains in his book *Comic Book Culture* that most alternative comics sell a lot less than mainstream comics.[34] He writes that most comics readers are adolescent men, while the alternative crowd tends to be composed of college students and has a larger share of female readers (about 40 percent). Pustz describes alternative readers in the following manner:

> Many readers of alternative comics come to them from alternative culture: these people listen to alternative music (a category as diverse as alternative comics), have non-conformist ideas regarding lifestyle, clothing, and personal appearance, and practice more liberal politics than most Americans. Most important though, is that most alternative-comics readers set themselves up in opposition to traditional mainstream American culture and to mainstream comic books. Aside of picking up a comic of *X-Men* for a few laughs, or buying an old issue of DC's *Superboy and the Legion of Superheroes* for its nostalgic value, most alternative-comic fans would not be caught dead reading mainstream comics.[35]

As an alternative creator who was impacted by the setup of the comic book distribution system, Gilbert Hernandez mocked the comic book retail system and how comics are disseminated. In the segment "Letters from Venus," Venus (a precocious and highly intelligent girl) goes to Shredder Records, an alternative record store, with her Japanese American schoolmate/friend Yoshio. In this type of punk/grunge retailer, all the alternative and antiestablishment comic books are featured on the stands as opposed to the superhero comics that tend to dominate the conventional stores. In the art of the page, one can distinguish eccentric titles on the stands of Shredder Records, such as Jaime Hernandez's *Penny Century* and *Whoa, Nelly!*, Peter Bagge's *Hate*, and Daniel Clowes's *Eightball*, which were some of the most trendy comics at the time in the American industry.[36] Yoshio laughs when, in a self-reflexive meta-narrative, he grabs a copy of Gilbert Hernandez's own *Grip*, which Venus dismisses as boring porn. The hipster employee at the store does not allow the two youngsters to continue perusing the comic because they are under age, but on the next page he catches them in the street and gives Venus a free copy

Venus receives a free copy of Gilbert Hernandez's Grip. Gilbert Hernandez, *Luba and Her Family*, 24.
© Gilbert Hernandez.

of *Grip* because, as he admits, he acted as "some old liquor store owner."[37]
This scene is important for my discussion in this chapter of the book, as it
illustrates Gilbert Hernandez's awareness of the fact that his comics at the
time were part of an alternative scene that tried to bypass the market and
economic limitations imposed on erotic and transgressive material.

In a later segment, "Letters from Venus: Life on Mars," Venus again encounters the employee from the store at a costume-themed carnival, and he
asks her why she hasn't visited his store again. Venus replies that she and her
mom Petra now go to the Winkydinky comic book store because it is closer
to her house.[38] Venus explains that her mother Petra does not want her to
visit the alternative store because it is "stinky punk" and sells the comics
Venus likes but cannot read due to her young age, while Winkydinky sells
the superhero comics her mother enjoys.[39] All of these events become further
infused with irony when in the segment "Letters from Venus: Who Cares
About Love," it is revealed that Petra is having an extramarital affair with
the Shredder Records employee in the backroom of the store.[40] This could be
interpreted as a jab at the hypocrisy of the system in which Venus is being
pushed to move from the "alternative space" to shop at the "wholesome and
kid-friendly" comic book store. This spatial displacement means that children
and teenagers are forced to consume infantile narratives and to veer away
from the sexuality and erotic appeal of the content sold in Shredder Records.
Meanwhile, Venus's mother as an adult is allowed to indulge and explore
sexuality and extramarital affairs in the same space that is denied to Venus.

Introduction

Los Bros Hernandez belonged to the late 1970s/early '80s California punk scene, which also made them part of the alternative music crowd at the time. They no longer participate in this punk scene, but following this type of lifestyle at the beginning of their careers certainly made them more rebellious than the typical comic book artists. As Charles Hatfield writes, "Specifically, Jaime and Gilbert evoked Southern California's punk rock scene, capturing its rough-and-tumble nature while applying its DIY (do-it-yourself) aesthetic to their own work."[41] Therefore their interests in this music's worldview led them to be self-sufficient and create material that evolved from the underground comix from the 1960s and mid-1970s rather than traditional adventures that would be published at Marvel or DC. Like Pustz's description of the alternative comics reader that I previously quoted, Los Bros tried to stay away from traditional storytelling, while sometimes intertextually indulging in the language and visual narratives of mainstream comics to parody them ironically in funny ways that are attractive to alternative readers. Charles Hatfield describes their work outside of the mainstream and comix frame:

> In addition, Los Bros defied the longstanding masculine bias of comic books by focusing on distinctive and complex female characters. These characters, as they matured, mixed caricature, low-key realism, and a refreshingly inclusive sense of beauty. As such, they broke with the fetishism of both mainstream adventure comics, with their feverish celebration of the disciplined, superheroic body, and most underground comix, with their scabrous, at times misogynistic sexual satire. The brothers' thematic innovations—the punk milieu, their eagerness to explore their Latino roots, and their regard for women—inspired fierce loyalty among their readers.[42]

Los Bros, under the leadership of older brother Mario, published the first issue of the anthology *Love and Rockets* with a low print run of 800 numbers.[43] Gilbert sent the issue to *The Comics Journal* for review, hoping to get some publicity even if the editors hated it.[44] The move paid off when publisher Gary Groth saw the potential in their anthology and decided to distribute their comic through his company Fantagraphics Books, which at the time also distributed *The Comics Journal*.[45] The brothers made an agreement with Fantagraphics, which allowed them to keep the publication rights of their works and to avoid editorial interference, as they would still be involved in every facet of their art (pencils, inks, and lettering). However, the company would help to promote them and would deal with the publishing minutiae, including matters of advertising, licensing, and distribution, which can be very distracting and time consuming for creators.

Under the Fantagraphics label, Los Bros Hernandez maintained a stable run for the first *Love and Rockets* series. They published 50 issues from 1981 to 1996, which were not best-sellers like the traditional superhero comics but which gained solid alternative-reader customer support and wide acclaim from reviewers and scholars. One aspect of their work that is important to acknowledge is that, by working outside of the mainstream publishing industry, they have been able to survive economically, as their lower print numbers remain profitable due to the fact that their financial gain is not designed to support megacorporations such as Marvel and DC Comics. In the bigger companies, comics selling lower than the top 100 are always in danger of being canceled because they are not seen as contributing to corporate profitability. Los Bros Hernandez's comics never crack the top 100, but they are never in danger of being canceled because their fan base is stable, never interested in gimmicks, and would even contribute to Los Bros' cause by buying multiple editions of the same storyline.

Complying with the Industry's Business Model

Even though Gilbert and Jaime Hernandez are independent/alternative creators, they still follow certain patterns of the comic book industry. For example, while many new readers only read their work in graphic novel collections that can be found in comic stores or national bookstores such as Amazon.com or Barnes and Noble, most of their material first appears in the thirty-two-page comic book format. Most of the industry's comic book companies follow this serial narrative model because by publishing in segments, they can profit faster from any series, and they assume that after they reprint the storyline in book format, fans will buy the material again because they will not want to bother reading from their comic collection. This means that a *Love and Rockets* fan would buy the comics because they cannot wait several years to see what happens next with their favorite Los Bros' characters, but then they would also buy the collection because it is easier to reread a book than to go through the individual issues again.

Many of these idiosyncrasies of the industry have certainly affected the publication of the Hernandez brothers' work. In an interview, Gilbert and Jaime mentioned that the reason they changed the original *Love and Rockets* magazine format to one similar to most traditional comics while launching the second volume was that retailers told them customers were complaining they could not fit *Love and Rockets* issues into their comic book boxes.[46] In addition, the brothers had stopped publishing the first anthology to create a series of spin-offs, such as Gilbert Hernandez's *Luba* (1998–2004) and *Luba's*

Comics and Stories (2000–2006), and Jaime's *Penny Century* (1997–2000). Many fans did not know these comics existed because the mainstream companies inundate the market and it becomes very difficult to know everything that can be ordered. It was easier for the Hernandez brothers to just publish everything under a second volume of *Love and Rockets* (2001–2007) and simply tell the customer to order the new issues of one single comic in the store.[47]

A third change in format occurred when Los Bros relaunched a third volume of the series (from 2008). Gilbert and Jaime realized that many of their readers were buying the majority of their books from online retailers and bookstores. Therefore, instead of publishing single issues of the series (mostly sold in comic and alternative record stores) to be later collected and sold in bookstores, they decided to turn *Love and Rockets* into a graphic novel series that comes out once a year but that features a larger page count and launches on the direct market and at book retailers at the same time. The series now also premieres each issue on tablet/smartphone applications at the time of its publication in hard copy, thus making it available in the entire country simultaneously.

Today, the distribution of comics has changed in such a manner that now Los Bros' books can be purchased in both mainstream and alternative bookstores. In addition, as of 2013, Fantagraphics has opened a new digital venue for them through the comiXology application. Now all the Hernandez's work can be bought at any time and any place with an Internet connection, and their art can be better appreciated on devices such as the iPad. On these new electronic devices, the reader can zoom into each individual comic panel in order to appreciate better the intricacies of the creators' pencils and inks. Now the reader can have direct access to Los Bros' work and does not need a mediator with a physical space, as it used to be in the past with the newsstands, comic book stores, and alternative "hipster-distribution system." I think this is the time for their work to be disseminated on a mainstream level and to truly enter other spheres of influence.

Since Los Bros Hernandez are one of the main research subjects in my academic career, I have read almost every single thing they have published and that is available. I have bought back issues on eBay, hardcover collections, smaller-format reprintings, iPad digital copies on comiXology, and old *Love and Rockets* merchandise. I have become as obsessed with their work as I am with my *Batman* collection, which is odd, considering one is not supposed to associate their work with crass consumption. To become a fan of Los Bros' works can be a daunting task because it involves reading thousands of comic book pages and remembering a complex continuity that can be as rough as knowing all the tidbits about Marvel Comics' *X-Men*. Scholar Derek Parker Royal comments on this complex collecting and reading phenomenon when he adds that it is likely one of the obstacles to integrating Gilbert and Jaime's comics in the classroom:

> One of the barriers to reading superhero titles is that if you are not already familiar with the "Marvel Universe" or the "DC Universe," it will be nearly impossible to grasp fully a story or narrative arc within a particular title. The publication history or backstory related to a DC or Marvel superhero, along with the backstories of the other heroes linked in some way to that subject, is vast and quite intimidating. Where is the narrative point of entry? How much can you truly comprehend by just jumping in, especially without referring to some kind of encyclopedic supplement . . . which itself could become a time-consuming endeavor? These are probably the same kind of questions confronting potential readers of *Love and Rockets*. When both fans and scholars look at the title's longevity, especially as given expression through Jaime's Locas stories or Gilbert's Palomar narratives, they may not see individual and graspable texts, but smaller and incomplete pieces of a much larger, even arabesque, tapestry. In the face of such a sprawling and intimidating body of work, how easy is it to devote a single critical essay or part of a class syllabus to a storyline from *Love and Rockets*, or even one of the many satellite graphic novels that circle the ongoing series? If we admit our uneasiness with "just jumping in," or our uncertainty in grasping the entirety of the brothers' output, then the paucity of scholarship begins to make more sense.[48]

The two main massive storylines that are part of the *Love and Rockets* anthology are Gilbert Hernandez's *Palomar* and Jaime Hernandez's *Locas*. Gilbert Hernandez's *Palomar* saga originally took place in a small and geographically undisclosed town in Central America. The story did not have a main protagonist, focusing instead on the residents of the town. Among the most interesting stories in this saga are "Heartbreak Soup," which introduced the town of Palomar, and the critically acclaimed "Human Diastrophism," which deals with art, politics, and a serial killer on the loose in the town. However, readers have to understand that to really appreciate the nuances of a particular segment of the story, they have to have read the entire *Palomar* saga. What could help the reader acquire the necessary background is the fact that Fantagraphics has made the whole series available in two cheaper volumes called *Heartbreak Soup* and *Human Diastrophism*. Collectors can also buy the whole narrative in one hardcover volume titled *Palomar: The Heartbreak Stories.*

During the *Palomar* storyline in the first run of *Love and Rockets*, the highly sexualized character of Luba began to gain more prominence and popularity. Gilbert revealed her origin in the critically acclaimed *Poison River* storyline, which was confusing to readers while it was being serialized but has now been better appreciated once it was collected as a graphic novel, currently included in the Fantagraphics collection *Beyond Palomar*.[49] Toward the end of the first volume of *Love and Rockets*, Luba's family and some of their neighbors move to the United States, where they become financially successful.

After the cancelation of the first *Love and Rockets* anthology, Gilbert continued Luba's storyline in three series: first in *Luba* and *Luba's Comics and Stories*, and then in the second volume of *Love and Rockets*. These stories were collected in three *Luba* volumes (*Luba in America, Ofelia's Book,* and *Three Daughters*) and in one hardcover (*Luba*). While this storyline is not part of the *Palomar* saga, due to the self-referential nature of the work, it makes more sense if the reader has read all the previous material too. One could say that besides the great character development, one of Gilbert's most interesting choices with his saga is how he shifted the story from representing a Latino idyllic vision of small towns in Latin America (*Palomar*) to a funny parody of decadent Latino bourgeoisie and unbridled sexuality (*Luba*). I will still refer to Luba's stories in America as part of the *Palomar* saga in the same way that most *Star Trek* fans would call *The Next Generation, Deep Space Nine, Voyager,* and *Enterprise* part of the *Star Trek* universe and canon.

Luba. Gilbert Hernandez, *Beyond Palomar*, 179. © Gilbert Hernandez.

One of the most important characters developed by Gilbert Hernandez in his *Luba* saga is Fritz, Luba's half sister and homage to Robert Crumb's *Fritz the Cat*. She is another highly sexualized and controversial character, who begins her career as a therapist but then becomes a B-movie and low-budget genre-actress superstar. Fritz is a very prominent character in the *Luba* saga, but her stories are mostly collected in the volume *High Soft Lisp*. Currently, Gilbert is working predominantly on writing "graphic novels" out of Fritz's B movies, which include *Chance in Hell*, *The Troublemakers*, *Love and Shadows*. He also began to publish in 2013 another graphic novel showing Fritz's cinematic adaptation of the *Poison River* storyline *(María M)*.

Most of Gilbert's work has been distributed by Fantagraphics, but his prestige has allowed him to occasionally work with mainstream publishers. He published a small *Iron Man* story in the miniseries *Marvel Tales*, a monthly comic for DC that was canceled (*Yeah!*), a miniseries (*Grip*) and a graphic novel (*Sloth*) for Vertigo (a DC Comics mature imprint), as well as a few miniseries for Dark Horse (*Speak of the Devil*, *Citizen Rex*, and *Fatima: The Blood Spinners*). In various online interviews, Gilbert has revealed that he likes to publish occasionally in the bigger companies because they offer higher remuneration rates.[50] However, he is not completely happy with the experience due to the pressures of a fast publishing schedule that he cannot control. One of the examples quoted by Gilbert Hernandez is how he could not finish the graphic novel *Sloth* because the Vertigo offices would not wait for him anymore and the editor wanted a clearer narrative.[51] He says that while many readers thought he had achieved something profound because of the obscure resolution of the book, it really was not his intention to provide a vague ending; rather, he was pressed for time and couldn't finish the storyline.[52]

Jaime has had a similar yet different career path from Gilbert. His *Locas* saga follows the lives of Maggie and Hopey, two young Latinas who were part of the 1980s punk movement in the United States. Unlike Gilbert's *Palomar* universe, where many of the main characters have recently immigrated into the United States, Jaime's Latinos are not first-generation immigrants, and the plots follow their lives, adventures, and misadventures in love while they grow up and mature. One of the better descriptions comparing the two brothers' aesthetics was provided by Derek Parker Royal:

> Gilbert's art is less "realistic" and more expressive than his brothers'
> (especially in the case of Jaime), and as a result, his illustrations appear less
> sophisticated to some fans. (There have been occasional debates within the

Love and Rockets reader community as to which brother produces the best work, some arguing that while Jaime is a better artist, Gilbert is a better writer. However, many of these arguments are largely moot, based more on fan preference than on broad critical appreciation.) Gilbert's work is heavily influenced by the kind of comics he grew up reading, such as Jack Kirby and Charles Schulz. He has also noted the debt his art owes to Robert Crumb—older brother Mario introduced him to underground comix by smuggling a copy of *Zap* into the house—and this is especially apparent in Gilbert's depictions of sex, often explicit and outrageous. Jaime's illustrations reflect more of a clean-line style. His work has been particularly influenced by Dan DeCarlo—his characters are strikingly reminiscent of DeCarlo's *Archie* and "good girl" art—but also by Hank Ketcham's *Dennis* and Schulz's *Peanuts*. The impact of Kirby and Steve Ditko is also apparent, especially in Jaime's superhero comics.[53]

I would say the main difference between Gilbert's and Jaime's work is that Jaime has integrated more American comic book genres into the fabric of his *Locas* narrative. Maggie and Hopey's stories have presented science fiction, superheroes, wrestling, political adventures that somehow fit into the continuity established by Jaime and cannot be dismissed as dream sequences or other typical plot devices. Gilbert's narrative abounds in intertextual devices (for example, Fritz's movie adaptations of material previously published by Gilbert) and surrealist techniques, but Jaime's interconnects better with the American comic book industry and its comic readers. The beginning of the *Locas* saga has a science fiction bend, and the character of Penny Century is used to deconstruct the superhero narratives that have dominated the American industry. This intertextual playfulness allows the creator to develop in more detail some of the most critically acclaimed comic characters of all time.

Jaime's *Locas* saga has been published in the three volumes of *Love and Rockets* and a few miniseries such as *Penny Century* and *Whoa Nelly!* and the strip published by the *New York Times*. The *Locas* saga has been collected in two hardcovers, *Locas* and *Locas II*, and in five paperbacks, *Maggie the Mechanic*, *The Girl from H.O.P.P.E.R.S.*, *Perla La Loca*, *Esperanza*, and *Penny Century*. The saga resumed in the third volume of *Love and Rockets*, where it continues to this day and with no ending in sight. Just recently, Jaime's superhero adventure featuring Maggie and Penny Century has been collected in the volume *God and Science: The Return of the Ti-Girls*, adding another volume to the *Locas* saga. Jaime's freelance work has reached some mainstream success. He has not been interested in doing too much work outside *Love and Rockets* and Fantagraphics, but he has done illustrations for the *New Yorker* and the prestigious home video company Criterion.

As of 2014, Gilbert and Jaime have maintained a high profile with their recent work. The more prolific Gilbert just released (in 2013) two hardcover collections of material he had previously published in *Love and Rockets* (*Julio's Day* and *Marble Season*), to a media blitz of rave reviews. The artist granted interviews to several national venues such as NPR and the *Chicago Tribune*, as his *Marble Season* received wide acclaim in the industry and reached the No. 2 position on *The New York Times* best-seller list. *Julio's Day* has recently become one of the best-reviewed graphic novels, an important feat considering the controversial gender and queer issues within an ethnic context that it openly addresses. Another original graphic novel, *Maria M* (2013), has also caught critics' and audiences' attention with its complex reinterpretation of earlier *Palomar* stories. Jaime provided the illustrations for Junot Díaz's short story collection *This Is How You Lose Her* and, in 2014, published *The Love Bunglers*, a collection of his new groundbreaking Maggie stories that appeared recently in *Love and Rockets*. One could argue that at this point, the brothers' work has reached a peak in sales, popularity, and outstanding critical reception.

spotlight 1

Marble Season:
Growing Up with Comics

MARBLE SEASON IS one of Gilbert Hernandez's most recent original graphic novels, and one of the few that was not published by Fantagraphics. Unlike the majority of Gilbert's other graphic novels, this one is a bildungsroman that does not feature one of Fritz's B movies. Instead, it follows the childhood experiences of three fictional Latino siblings and includes many events similar to what Los Bros have disclosed in interviews about the Hernandez family. By turning his real-life experience into fiction, Gilbert comments on the formation of comic book fandom in the 1950s and shows how reading habits were established and changed as a result of the changes that occurred in the comic book industry at the time.

The main character of the story is Huey, a Latino child, who is introduced to comics by his older brother Junior. The latter, while waiting to get a haircut, reads the copies lent to him by his barber. It is obvious that these comics are not yet seen as collectibles, so the covers are torn and the comics are generally in bad shape (5). Junior and Huey, however, begin to collect comics (especially monster comics), and their tastes are self-reflexively similar to Mario's and Gilbert's, respectively (37, 44). Throughout the story, Gilbert comments on several aspects of comic culture, such as the ideological change of the American enemies (from Nazis to Communists) (45) and the surge of horror comics in the 1950s (63). He even mentions the transformation of adult comics into magazines as a strategy to escape the Comics Code, when one of Huey's friends introduces him to *Creepy* (92–93). This particular story has so many allusions to the pop culture of the 1950s and '60s that its publisher Drawn & Quarterly included a series of endnotes to explain the outdated references to contemporary readers, who may not be knowledgeable about the history of fan culture (126).

The importance of the story is that it narrates the birth of fan culture from a Latino point of view and shows how that culture helped to integrate a Latino family into American society. Gilbert is conscious of some of the racist undertones in American society at the time, as, for example, when the other kids nickname Huey "Captain Mexican" instead of Captain America (14–18). Nevertheless, Huey later befriends Anglo kids who also collect comics and thus comes into contact with a multiethnic fan culture that unites diverse strands of American society. At the end of the story, as Huey begins his passage into adulthood, he is somewhat anxious about the future yet looks forward to a new stage in his life: "I guess what can be scary sometimes is thinking about what it will be like in the future. I just hope I like being a grownup." (120)

chapter one

Subverting the Intertextual
Comic Book Corporate Structure

THE WORKS OF Gilbert and Jaime Hernandez are critically acclaimed and generally well received inside and outside of the comic industry, but it is a challenge for casual readers to truly appreciate the intricacies of their work. The ideal reader would know how the comic book visual language works, would have some background knowledge about the material that has been published before in the American industry, and would be familiar with some basic aspects of Latino culture in the United States. The epic narrative scope of the Hernandez's oeuvre, with its subversive sexuality, playful use of genre tropes, and complex Latino characters with varied ethnic and gender signifiers may overwhelm novice and experienced readers alike.

The intertextual tapestry that Los Bros Hernandez have created throughout their careers can be very challenging, and its interpretation would depend on the individual reader's background and worldview. The situation is further complicated by the late arrival of comic books into the (high school and college) curriculum in the United States. For, even if many readers are taught how to analyze or interpret literature—for example, plays, poetry, novels, and so forth—the majority still would have no training in comic book analysis or interpretation. That is why I believe it would be difficult for some readers to grasp the symbiotic relationship between a traditional mainstream and corporate comic book narrative language and the aesthetics of ethnic and alternative artists such as Gilbert and Jaime Hernandez.

In this chapter I will explore the idea of intertextuality and its theoretical conceptualization and apply it to a sample of Los Bros Hernandez's work. I will specifically explore concepts such as parody, appropriation, and pastiche, which are very relevant in my discussion of some of Gilbert and Jaime's main influences from both mainstream (Harvey Kurtzman's *Mad*) and alternative comic creators (Robert Crumb and others). While examining intertextual devices that have helped to form the brothers' nonhegemonic narratives, I will provide an in-depth analysis of some segments of the first issue of *Love and Rockets*, specifically Gilbert's "BEM," and Jaime's "Penny Century, You're Fired" and "Mechanics." These stories were particularly important because they established the narrative displacements of previous comic book genres where Los Bros' ambitious epics *Palomar* and *Locas* germinated. I will also explore the importance of Jaime's Penny Century character in the *Locas* saga and especially the recently published storyline that launched its third volume, "The Return of the Ti-Girls." Penny's character provides an insight into the philosophy of *Love and Rockets*, as it demonstrates how Los Bros' artistry and narratives simultaneously comply and clash with the hegemonic corporate structures in an American comic book industry focused on the superhero genre.

Comic Book Authors and Intertextuality

Narrative intertextuality is an ambiguous and complex theoretical concept that scholars have been trying to define in the twentieth and twenty-first centuries. The beginnings of its definition can be traced to some of the structuralist linguistic concepts developed by Ferdinand de Saussure, through which he sought to explore signs and their connection to meaning. Later, Saussure's theories evolved into a more nuanced cultural debate with the writings of Soviet scholar Mikhail Bakhtin and French-Bulgarian Julia Kristeva, who incorporated the concept of ambivalence (created by different social situations) into the meaning of linguistic signs, thus marking the beginning of the poststructuralist period.[1] Kristeva herself coined the term "intertextuality" in her work and, according to Graham Allen, it became widespread when she introduced the work of Mikhail Bahktin in essays such as "The Bounded Text" and "Word, Dialogue, and Novel."[2] This theoretical concept is still used in modern academia to analyze literary and narrative devices that express the fluidity, interconnectedness, and shiftiness of meaning.

According to scholar Frank D'Angelo, among the most important concepts in intertextual criticism are adaptation, retro/nostalgia, appropriation, parody, pastiche, and simulation. D'Angelo defines adaptation as the process of "recasting of a rhetorical text into a new form," retro/nostalgia as a narrative with "an idealized longing for the past," and appropriation as "a rhetorical device of borrowing from and copying other works."[3] The other concepts (parody, pastiche, and simulation) are more broad and debated, as they employ adaptation, nostalgia, and appropriation to recreate previous ideas through a new form. In my analysis, I will emphasize parody and pastiche, which are essential to any discussion of Gilbert and Jaime's graphic storytelling, since both artists are excellent representatives of the self-reflexive postmodern age that is linked with poststructuralism. To describe Los Bros' oeuvre, I would use Linda Hutcheon's definition of the postmodern narrative as "fiction that is at once metafictional and historical in its echoes of the texts and contexts of the past."[4]

This book is about the work of two American *auteurs*, but Los Bros' role in the creation of their comics would be downplayed by many cultural critics who have developed intertextual theory within the field of semiotics. The writings of Bakhtin and Kristeva opened a path for the groundbreaking work of French literary critic Roland Barthes and French philosopher Michel Foucault, both of whom de-emphasized the role of the author in the construction/shifting of meaning in texts. Barthes specifically explains that, "We know now that a text is not a line of words releasing a single 'theological' meaning (the 'message' of the Author-God) but a multi-dimensional space in which a variety of writings, none of them original, blend and clash. The text is a tissue of quotations drawn from the innumerable centres of culture."[5] Foucault, in turn, specifically points out how previous "literary discourse was acceptable only if it carried an author's name" but "auteurship" is not always needed to read a text.[6]

Barthes and Foucault opposed the traditional literary criticism, which used the author as the creator and authoritarian provider of meaning. In his seminal 1967 essay "The Death of the Author," Barthes uses Balzac's description and gender perception of a castrato in the short story "Sarrasine" to debate if these were the French author's own views or a representation of how his society at the time perceived certain ideas.[7] While Barthes's views of authorship have been very influential, according to scholar Graham Allen some contemporary cultural critics are currently defending the relevancy of the author in narrative intertextuality, specifically when dealing with feminist and ethnic literature.[8] In these particular cases, the role and experience of the author may be relevant in creating new cultural and formalistic innovations in the narrative that defy a monolithic canon that had previously excluded them. Allen specifically refers to Nancy K. Miller, who criticizes the poststructuralist dismissal of the author "in favor of the (new) monolith of anonymous textuality, or in Focault's phrase, 'transcendental anonymity.'"[9]

Gilbert and Jaime's role as authors is important to acknowledge in my study of the intertextual connections they employ. Their narratives contain allusions, parodies, appropriations, and other intertextual devices that frequently serve as an intersection of influences from hegemonic mainstream comic book narratives (monsters, melodrama, superheroes) and the ironic subaltern identity that comes from their relationship with the comic book underground movement, alternative comics, and their Latino/Mexican heritage. One of the best examples of an intertextual reference where Gilbert questions the meaning of traditional elements in American popular culture appears in his *Palomar* storyline. In one of the segments, the character Venus is discussing the popular TV character Spock with her aunt Fritz, who is also a science fiction fan. In this particular story, Venus, who has just watched *Star Trek* for the first time, asks her aunt why the "hillbilly doctor" (Dr. McCoy) is so racist to the half-Vulcan, half-human Spock.[10]

Star Trek is a very popular TV show with American comic book readers (especially those of Gilbert's generation), and it is showcased by its studio (Paramount) as an example of the representation of a utopian society and a groundbreaking series in terms of race. For the most part, sci-fi genre fans have internalized this idea in their subculture. However, if a contemporary viewer watches the show through the lens of modern political correctness, it is very obvious that Dr. McCoy displays racist behavior toward Spock. His problematic attitudes, as Venus observes, include constant references to Spock's green blood as a shortcoming and sarcastic remarks about his Vulcan heritage. The character of Captain James T. Kirk, who represents authority, stays away from the squabbles that occur between McCoy and Spock, something that Venus criticizes, as she is accustomed to modern authority figures who punish racist behavior. This is why she says to one of her friends that Captain Kirk should fire Dr. McCoy.[11]

As a character with blond hair and a Latino background, Venus identifies with Spock's existentialist link to his biracial heritage and sees the doctor as a racist white individual whom she specifically associates with the derogatory term "hillbilly." One does not have to be Latino/a or biracial to understand or identify with Spock's internal conflict, but it is obvious that Gilbert (through Venus) presents his own views of how *Star Trek* can be problematic from a

Venus discusses *Star Trek* character Spock with her aunt Fritz. Gilbert Hernandez, *Luba and Her Family*, 91. © Gilbert Hernandez.

modern perspective, specifically when seen through the point of view of a biracial or simply inquisitive person, who would perceive a genre canonical text in a way different from what its established reading would offer. However, as his article "What Is an Author?" would suggest, a critic such as Foucault would not agree with the idea of focusing on Gilbert's ethnic authorial agency, in other words, with the suggestion that he understands these ideas because he himself is a Latino author. This is because antiracist discourse can originate in different cultural strands that form the message present in the text.[12] Thus, while I plan to focus my analysis based on Jaime and Gilbert's authorship of the texts, I will also reference different texts that have created the cultural background in which Los Bros operate.

It is difficult to apply intertextual theory to comic book authors (even though comic book culture is very interconnected) because many of the foundational texts, from Bakhtin to Barthes, have been written by literary scholars who study almost exclusively the written prose. For example, Bakhtin's idea of dialogism and the clashing of voices and discourses within the text was originally used by the Russian scholar to discuss the power of the novel as a narrative medium that can challenge official discourse (see *Problems of Dostoevsky's Poetics*). However, current scholars such as Linda Hutcheon (*A Theory of Adaptation*) and Robert Stam (*Literature and Film: A Guide to the Theory and Practice of Film Adaptation*) have begun to apply the concepts of intertextuality to different mediums such as cinema and even amusement parks, proving that the idea of connections and self-reference can also be applied outside of traditional literature or prose.

One of the problems some readers may have when transferring intertextual concepts from literature to other narrative mediums is a lack of understanding of how these new mediums work. For example, most of my students have barely read any comic strips in the course of their young lives. As a result, they often struggle even with the basics (such as reading the order of the visual sequence) and become lost within the visual structure of the comic page. Some may have read graphic novels that have made it into the high school English canon, such as Art Spiegelman's *Maus*, but the majority confirm that their English instructors tend to emphasize the Holocaust plot and the words of the author in the discussion, rather than teach the students how to appreciate the visual compositions of the page. It is important to acknowledge in the classroom the visual structure of the comic and its evolution throughout the twentieth century because it affects the interpretation of the author's message and visual allusions. This is why, in order to understand Los Bros Hernandez's oeuvre, besides understanding the basic plot of their stories, one must also have a sense of how they visually communicate their ideas and their connections to other artists from the past.

One of the most important books to deal with issues relevant to comic book intertextuality is Scott McCloud's *Understanding Comics*. His book is designed to make comic and non-comic readers alike understand how the comic book images and text work together to provide a narrative that is unique and different to prose and to other types of visual narratives such as animation and live-action cinema. McCloud's ideas about comic art fit the poststructuralist period because he specifically describes how artists can utilize iconography along with traditional prose to display different moods and emotions that comic readers, savvy and experienced with the medium, know how to interpret.[13] His book introduces novice readers to the basic visual tools and styles and other storytelling devices through which authors convey action, speed, emotion.[14] Scholar Charles Hatfield, who has written about the difficulties of comic reading, explains further that "The fractured surface of the comics page, with its patchwork of different images, shapes, and symbols, presents the reader with a surfeit of interpretive options, creating an experience that is always decentered, unstable, and unfixable."[15]

However, even though "comic book language" is full of visual icons and devices that have been recycled throughout centuries of publication, it is still difficult to completely remove the author from the narrative. The most prestigious comic book artists have a particular auteurist style in their comics because, in contrast to prose storytellers who rely on their specific use of a spoken/written language, comic book artists are also defined by their individual visual style. Their drawing techniques may have been influenced by artistic tools they have appropriated from other artists, but in some cases their drawings have unique qualities that make them visually recognizable to any experienced comic book fan. In the case of Los Bros Hernandez, one could say that their drawings have a distinct style to the point that any experienced *Love and Rockets* reader could distinguish who drew a particular story in the anthology by just looking at the images.[16]

It is important to point out that the tools that Gilbert and Jaime use to manipulate their images and to elicit reactions from the comic reader have been developed in the American comic industry during most of the twentieth and twenty-first centuries. As a consequence, readers will undoubtedly perceive the brothers' art and stories in relationship to other comics that are being published. For example, when Jaime draws super heroines in the *Locas* saga, most experienced readers will compare his visuals to what is being published in mainstream companies like Marvel and DC Comics. They will accept some conventional tropes that he re-creates but they will also take notice of specific unique details, such as when he draws the character of Angel as a superhero with an obese body structure. This could be perceived as a funny visual transgression of the genre and the well-known fact that comic book companies tend to depict women with unrealistic physiques.

Los Bros Hernandez's ethnic Latino upbringing may at times add another layer of intertextuality. In his *Poison River* storyline, Gilbert provides an example when he mocks the controversial Mexican minstrel cartoon character Memín Pinguín with his parodic creation Pedro Pacotilla. This is a very interesting case because it can show how different readers can react to the same iconography that Gilbert is parodying. In his comprehensive chapter about *Palomar*, renowned comic book scholar Charles Hatfield discusses in depth the character of Pedro Pacotilla as a criticism of the tradition of racist comics and lowbrow mass culture. However, he does not mention one single time how the character is based on Yolanda Vargas Dulché and Sixto Valencia's *Memín Pinguín*, the original Mexican source of Gilbert's parody. Yet the visual allusion to Memín, an iconic Mexican comic book character, would be easily recognized by Mexican (and many U.S. Latino) readers, even if they are not necessarily well-versed in Vargas Dulché's work.

Because I read the entire run of *Memín* in the 1980s when I was a child, I initially thought that Gilbert had a hidden criticism embedded in the story and that it should be explored further in my research with the possible goal of expanding on what Hatfield had already written. However, when I interviewed Gilbert, he confirmed that Pedro is a parody of Memín but admitted that he had never read any of the comics because he does not know Spanish. This was an important statement, as it meant he was just mocking the racist idea of the Mexican character but not the original Mexican narrative. He had access to the comic because he was Mexican American, but his critique could not be about the comic series' plot because he did not understand the words on the page. If one reads *Poison River* and analyzes the character of Pedro Pacotilla in more detail, it is obvious that the art Gilbert uses for the parody does not actually correspond to the one found in Memín. My Hispanic background had made me see more into Pedro's character than the author intended, and my interview with Gilbert also made me realize the simplicity of his criticism. At the end, as Hatfield writes in his book, Gilbert is just mocking the general idea of "sambo" icons as a representation of racism but not necessarily parodying Yolanda Vargas Dulché's narrative structure and visual techniques.

The ironic references and parodic style in Gilbert and Jaime's comics can be traced to American artists from the past such as Harvey Kurtzman and Robert Crumb. Some academics such as Charles Hatfield and Roger Sabin have established the connections between the comix movement that defied the Comics Code Authority on the one hand and the alternative artists (such as Los Bros) that thrived with the rise of the direct-market distribution system on the other. In the next section, I explore the legacy of Kurtzman and Crumb and how it influenced the Hernandez brothers' styles—specifically, the idea of comic book parody that was so important when launching *Love and Rockets*.

Intertextual Parody: The Influence of Harvey Kurtzman in the 1950s and the Later Underground Comix Movement

Los Bros Hernandez publish most of their books through Fantagraphics, a company that was the home of *The Comics Journal*. As I mentioned in the introduction, the company specializes in promoting some of the best alternative contemporary comic book and graphic novel creators (Gilbert and Jaime, as well as others, such as Daniel Clowes) and reprinting prestigious authors from the past (for example, Harvey Kurtzmann, Carl Barks, and Robert Crumb) that influenced the more artful comics from the modern age.[17] As Fantagraphics officially distributes many of the important works of these comic auteurs, this publishing label has become well respected within academia because of how it has presented the cultural and aesthetic connections between these legendary comic book writers/artists. Specifically, the company has emphasized the evolution of the different anti-system writers within the industry, from Harvey Kutzman's parodies in *Mad* magazine to the critical and more nihilist appropriations of the underground comix movement (with Robert Crumb as a figurehead) that set up the scene for alternative creators such as Los Bros Hernandez.

This lineage promoted by *The Comics Journal* (Kurtzman, Crumb, Los Bros) has been questioned by the artists themselves. For example, even though Los Bros acknowledge the importance of Kurtzman's *Mad* in their careers, Gilbert finds unfair that editor Gary Groth constantly promotes Kurtzman, who is a humorist, at the expense of others.[18] In an interview with Groth, Gilbert asserts, "Because sometimes you guys would like stuff, like Harvey Kurtzman; but I thought, Harvey Kurtzman draws like a funny guy. And [*Journal* critics] hated the guy from *Epic*, the guy who used to draw mashed potatoes, Tim Conrad."[19] Further, even though Gilbert adores Robert Crumb, he does not agree with the latter's depiction of women.[20] On the other hand, Crumb himself has some problems with Los Bros' comics, as he thinks Jaime's women are too idealized and Gilbert's narratives have become too frivolous.[21] Still, besides their differences in approach and philosophy, what all these creators have in common is their central place in the study of the role of parody in American comics.

Kurtzman, Crumb, and Los Bros Hernandez employ many self-referential techniques in their comics. As mentioned at the beginning of this chapter, a useful classification of intertextual devices is offered by Frank D'Angelo, who categorizes them into adaptation, parody, retro, appropriation, and pastiche. When discussing adaptation in particular, scholar Linda Hutcheon stipulates that for adaptation to work there must be a direct relationship between two texts (adapted and adapting), and the adapted text is something both acknowledged and recognizable.[22] Adaptations are thus tricky in the comic book industry due to copyright issues, so direct adaptations of modern material (recent novels, films, other comics) have to be officially sanctioned by the corporations that own the respective character. The preferred method of intertextuality for modern comic book artists tends to be the idea of appropriation because it allows the artists to legally adopt drawing techniques, character archetypes, and genre narrative structures from other artists, which they continue to develop into more exciting new narratives that present more contemporary visions of reality. Scholar Julie Sanders describes the concept of appropriation in literary studies in the following manner:

> Appropriation frequently affects a more decisive journey away from the informing source into a wholly new cultural product and domain. This may or may not involve a generic shift, and it may still require the intellectual

juxtaposition of (at least) one text against another that we have suggested is central to the reading and spectating experience of adaptations. But the appropriated text or texts are not always as clearly signaled or acknowledged as in the adaptive process.[23]

Appropriations techniques were essential in the art of Harvey Kurtzman, one of the forefathers of the underground comix movement and alternative comics. During the turbulent years that led to the creation of the Comics Code Authority, he was arguably one of the main artists who challenged, within the industry's parameters, the genres embedded through constant repetition into the American culture industry of the time. In the comprehensive book *The Art of Harvey Kurtzman: The Mad Genius of Comics*, comic book historians Denis Kitchen and Paul Buhle collect several interviews that explain that the artist's subversive qualities were initially present in his antiracist and anti-war work in the different anthologies published by EC comics.[24] However, Kurtzman is best known for his work in the legendary comic *Mad* that was originally also published by EC, and which has been recognized as one of the most important sources of satire and parody regarding American popular culture. The success of the comic led to Kurtzman's being able to transform the title into the magazine known today, a move that allowed *MAD* to escape the economic censorship brought about by the Comics Code Authority.

Kurtzman left the magazine after several issues because of some financial disagreements with the publisher, but the title is still published today and is constantly quoted in American media. I have been subscribed to *MAD* for several decades, and I enjoy how the magazine continues to deploy Kurtzman's deconstruction of the American entertainment industry and popular culture, from "serious" projects such as *Game of Thrones* to important politicians such as George Bush and Barack Obama. However, to be in on the joke or the criticism, one needs to know the references in order for the parody to make sense. When I read some of Kurtzman's early parodies in *Mad* (reprinted in the 1990s), I did not get a lot of the humor because I was not familiar with the English slang of his time, I was not aware of the controversies happening in the American comic book industry in the 1950s, and I did not understand his specific ironic wit.[25]

The idea of parody is so complex that it can be traced all the way to ancient times, as Linda Hutcheon did in her book *A Theory of Parody*. There are several points the scholar makes in her writing that are relevant to my further discussion of comic artists such as Kurtzman, Crumb, and Los Bros Hernandez. One of the most important elements of her discussion is the difference she establishes between satire and parody, even though she claims that the two terms may converge in certain texts. For Hutcheon, satire has a "disdainful ethos" that parodies lack. According to her, many parodies today do not ridicule the background texts but use them as standards by which to place the contemporary ones under scrutiny. Therefore, parodic art both deviates from an aesthetic norm and includes that norm within itself as background material. Hutcheon adds that "[p]arody is, then, an important way for modern artists to come to terms with the past—through ironic recoding or, in my awkward descriptive neologism, "trans-contextualizing."[26]

One of the most important and vintage canonical parodies in the American comic book industry is Harvey Kurtzman and Wally Wood's "Superduperman." This story appeared in the fourth issue of *Mad,* which at the time was published by the controversial company EC comics. In the first three issues, the parody used was very broad, and generally mocking EC's horror line. "Superduperman" was the first time they were subverting specific texts from other companies that the reading audience would recognize. Kurtzman was able to parody DC's *Superman* and Fawcett's *Captain Marvel* because he was able to find a legal loophole in which "parody" is protected by the First Amendment.[27] The legality and importance of parody is validated by Linda Hutcheon when she states specifically that the difference between parody and plagiarism clearly involves the issue of intent, as both are acknowledged borrowings, but the plagiarist "conceal[s] rather than engage the decoder in the interpretation of their backgrounded texts."[28] Hutcheon believes that irony is the main element needed in parodies to reconceptualize an older text.[29]

This "Superduperman" story was important because in it, Kurtzman was able to deconstruct the silliness of the superhero comics that would later become the hegemonic genre in the American comic book industry. He had to change the names of the superheroes from Superman to Superduperman and from Captain Marvel to Captain Marbles, and he could not use the trademarked Superman shield that appears on the character's chest. Nevertheless, he was able to subvert the conventions of the genre by portraying the two models of American superhero masculinity as two destructive physical forces that are pathetic in their handling of women. In a particular Wally Wood drawing, Superduperman is presented as a pervert while he peeks into the ladies' room at his newspaper office.[30] This irreverent joke disrupts the superhero idealism of the 1950s and made the parody very attractive for comic book readers at the time, as it questions the sexual purity of the superheroes in that time period (under the supervision of the Comics Code Authority).

Kurtzman and Wood's take on Superman and Captain Marvel sounds like a mean parody, but it was so well received in the industry that *Mad* became a smash success. Its influence is deemed essential to the development of comic book language in the American industry, and the best example is its impact on Alan Moore's *Watchmen*. In an interview for *Entertainment Weekly*, Moore declares that *Mad* was "the best comic ever." He adds further that his legendary *Watchmen*, in which he parodies the superheroes of the publishing company Charlton Comics, was a serious take on what Kurtzman and Wood had accomplished in "Superduperman."[31] This shows the importance of parody, as the questioning of the superhero aesthetics (and business practices) in Kurtzman's text was essential in the development of *Watchmen*, one of the greatest superhero stories of all time.

Even though the Superduperman story plays an important part in the history of comic books, it would be impossible to predict a contemporary reader's reaction to it in a modern context. While experienced modern readers can appreciate Kurtzman's deformations of the superhero genre and art, there are certain cultural subtexts they could not possibly understand. When discussing parody, Linda Hutcheon explains that while "parody offers a much more limited and controlled version of this activation of the past by giving it a new and often ironic context, it makes similar demands upon the reader, but these are demands more on his or her openness to play."[32] Kurtzman's story, besides mocking the superhero genre, also had a metaphorical historical allusion to the lawsuit in which DC Comics sued Fawcett over supposedly plagiarizing their trademarked Superman with their Captain Marvel creation.[33] This fact may be known to readers from the time that the comic was published, or to those who are aware of the history of the comic book industry. Still, individual readers will never interpret the text in the same way because they have different background knowledge. A perfect reader does not exist, which is why scholar Goran Hermerén writes that "if the notion of allusion is defined in terms of the reaction of ideal readers, a normative element is inevitably introduced, since these readers will define the proper way of understanding the text in question."[34]

Readers may be interested in parodies for different reasons. One of the most interesting projects that Fantagraphics has released is *The Sincerest Form of Parody*, a collection of some of the comedic comic books inspired by *Mad* in the 1950s. Because Kurtzman's *Mad* comic was a best-seller on the stands, other companies from his time sought to profit from his success and release new series that spoofed mainstream American comics and popular culture. John Benson, the editor of the book, collected some of the best material in these comics to demonstrate the influence of Kurtzman on the industry of the time, but also to show how the intertextual aspects of the parody differed with other creators. For example, one of the strips included is a satire of Harold Gray's famous strip *Little Orphan Annie* by Karl Hubber.[35] Benson mentions that Hubber's parody would have been released at the same time of Kurtzman's, but its printing was delayed. However, although both artists mock the conservative values of the original strip, Benson mentions that Hubber aesthetically mocks the visuals of the comics because he uses the shading techniques of Harold Gray. This example represents the different types of intertextual elements that the artist could parody, which range from obvious visuals, concepts, and plot elements to just simply mimicking some visual techniques from the original texts that a more aesthetically oriented comic reader can grasp.

Kurtzman's legacy carried on with the continuing publication of *Mad* magazine by other creators, in the other comics directly inspired by his work, and in his posterior adult work in *Playboy* magazine. Scholar Roger Sabin writes about Kurtzman's important role:

> The underground was basically an American phenomenon, which was then imitated in Britain. It originated from a variety of sources, which can be traced back to the 1950s. First, and perhaps most importantly, there was the influence of the *Mad* tradition. Harvey Kurtzman had liberated comedy in comics with this seminal title: along with its more inventive imitators, it was to inspire a new generation of cartoonists to push back the boundaries of satire even further. More directly, in his post-*Mad* magazine *Help!*, Kurtzman provided pages devoted to "amateur talent," where many future undergrounders got their first break.[36]

One of the most important creators influenced by his work was underground comix pioneer Robert Crumb. This particular artist worked under Kurtzman and published a few stories in *Help!*[37] Crumb later pioneered the underground comix movement in San Francisco, which was able to bypass some of the distribution limitations on the stands (due to the Comics Code) by publishing in alternative venues, as I mentioned in the introduction. Charles Hatfield best explains how the comix movement and figures such as Crumb expanded the idea of irony and double meaning in the American comic book industry in his comments on Crumb's *Zap*:

> Crumb's efforts were inherently ironic, in a manner not unlike that of Pop artists before him. Indeed this is his signal contribution to American comics: the ironizing of the comic book medium itself. With *Zap*, Crumb

achieved something that had eluded Pop Art: he ironically usurped not only the content of comics (that is, the characters and situations he had imbibed from childhood onward) but also the format (the periodical comic book), achieving a union of form and content that Pop Art, ensconced within the fine art world, could not. Crumb's *Zap* represented a reflexive *comic-book* commentary on comic books unlike anything since the early days of *Mad* magazine (in its original comic book incarnation, 1951–55). Moreover, *Zap* was free of *Mad*'s bottom-line commercial ambitions.[38]

When Matthew Pustz wrote about Crumb's use of controversial sexuality, he mentioned "that although Crumb certainly was not above doing sex stories for their own sake, his explicit stories often had an element of satire behind them."[39] One example in which Crumb distorted the readers' expectations about American cartoon art was when in his *Fritz the Cat* comics he used the "cute animal critters" aesthetic device, traditionally employed by wholesome American companies, to portray the rebellious counterculture life. When we are introduced to Fritz, the feline protagonist, he returns home and has an incestuous fling with his sister. This explicit use of sexuality (and controversial misogynistic devices) certainly amused some of the consumers of Crumb's work who used to buy his comics because they represented a challenge to narratives that channeled hegemonic values. Kurtzman had begun the process with *Mad,* but Crumb's underground comix took the cultural and aesthetic challenge further because he was not limited by corporate morality.

It is important to point out that Fritz was Crumb's creation, and that with this character the artist was playing with a style and techniques used to support the hegemonic system. However, at some point the rampant appropriation and subversion employed by the comix movement was threatened by lawsuits, such as the case of *Walt Disney v. The Air Pirates.* The Pirates were a group of cartoonists who almost merged the idea of adaptation and appropriation by illegally using characters such as Mickey Mouse in their parodies that contained adult themes. Disney's lawsuit against the group brought up some important new developments in terms of adaptation. In the United States, parodies are legally protected under the First Amendment as a freedom of speech issue; however, in this case it seemed that what defines a legal adaptation and parody also involves other elements, such as trademark infringement and other legal hurdles. The trial affected the ways in which parodies and intertextual narratives are perceived and made in the United States because it established a difference between simply mocking/parodying an idea and actually profiting from that idea. In the case of Los Bros Hernandez, it is very obvious that they are intertextually parodying other texts while being very careful not to break any laws. As a result, their reference points are often obscure due to the mainstream corporations' constant vigilance over their properties.

The First Stories in *Love and Rockets: New Stories #1*: Gilbert's "BEM" and Jaime's "Mechan-X"

When attending fan conventions of any kind, I have noticed that one of the most frequently asked questions that tend to annoy a creator easily is, "What are your main influences?" Creators are often reluctant to answer this question because it could be interpreted as an accusation of not being original, and also because it is the fans' way of testing the creator's "geek credentials." In *The Art of Jaime Hernandez*, the author (Todd Hignite) asked Jaime in detail about the comics he read as a child, thus looking for intertextual connections to previous work. Among the comic strips mentioned were Carl Barks's *Uncle Scrooge*, Dan De Carlo's *Archie*, *Little Archie*, EC Comics' horror line, Marvel superheroes and many others, which as texts provide a variety of humor, action, and excitement.[40] Some critics see these comics as formative influences on Los Bros' work and have even remarked how the structure of Jaime's comics is a reflection of the structure of the *Archie* series. However, Los Bros' main goal in their narratives is not to directly quote or pay homage to other texts but rather to use some of the techniques and narrative devices they have encountered in the process of creating their respective original sagas.

Before addressing the groundbreaking elements of *Love and Rockets #1*'s postmodern take on comics, I wanted to go back to intertextual theory and discuss certain important elements of Bakhtin's ideas about dialogism and the novel. When the Russian critic discussed the novel (and especially important authors such as Dostoevsky), he praised this particular narrative type's ability to establish dissenting voices that comply or clash with the author's point of view. Bakhtin does not eradicate completely the author (as Barthes and Foucault did later), but he is aware of the writer/author's inability to completely control the discourse of all of the characters.[41]

In his book *Problems of Dostoevsky's Poetics*, Bakhtin discusses his influential idea of the carnivalesque that has become very relevant in postcolonial studies. The Russian author uses the metaphor of the carnival to express the idea of heteroglossia, where many points of view come together and clash right under the noses of the authority that sponsors the event. This idea is important in anti-hegemonic writing because it opens a space for new points of view inside the rigid literary structures. Bakhtin believed that the power of the novel lies in providing a venue for characters that represent views contrasting those of the author and the main character, which leads to a transcendental view of humanity as a whole. Bakhtin writes, "Self-consciousness as the dominant in the construction of a character's image requires the creation of an artistic atmosphere that would permit his discourse to reveal and illuminate itself. Not a single element in this atmosphere can be neutral: everything must touch the character to the quick, provoke him, interrogate him, even polemicize with him and taunt him; everything must be directed toward the hero himself, turned toward him, everything must make itself felt as discourse about someone actually present, as the word of a 'second' and not of a 'third' person."[42]

Bakhtin firmly believed that a literary device such as parody was not a blatant rejection but rather the rebirth of a particular genre or narrative. This is why one of his best examples illustrating his ideas is his analysis of Cervantes's *Don Quixote*. In this case, Cervantes parodied medieval novels about Christian knights but instead of simply dismissing this type of storytelling, he created a superior text that can exist due to the clashing perspectives in his novel. Every character in the novel clashes with the protagonist's outdated point of view, and through this process, he and the novel become the greatest knight and knight novel of all time, respectively.[43]

It is important to refer to Bakhtin before beginning to analyze *Love and Rockets* for, as mentioned previously, some of the plotlines such as Gilbert's *Palomar* and Jaime's *Locas* sagas have been published over a period of thirty years and have created longer and more complex narratives than most prose novels can achieve. As a result, the brothers' storylines are populated by many characters, and the stories have shifted directions so many times that it is often unclear who the main characters are. Even though some could say that Gilbert and Jaime emphasize Luba's family and Maggie, respectively, their protagonists' points of view are constantly questioned by secondary characters who bring in other conflicting perspectives.

When one reads Gilbert's "BEM" and Jaime's "Mechan-X," the first two stories published by Los Bros in the first issue of *Love and Rockets*, it is very important to be aware of how they are constructed to express different elements of the comic industry in a pastiche of comic genres, the juxtaposition of which served to function in a subversive alternative manner to what was published by mainstream American comic book companies at the time. Reading these stories in their original context (without knowing that Los Bros would be publishing more stories with some of the same characters) must have been

Introduction of a traditional hero in "BEM." Gilbert Hernandez, *Amor y Cohetes*, 12. © Gilbert Hernandez.

a strange experience for readers from that period because they had to interpret the intertextual baggage of the story with bizarre references and without knowing the direction the narrative would take in the following issues.

Pastiche is a type of intertextuality often deployed by postmodern authors that can sometimes overlap with our definitions of parody. In this type of narrative, the author uses different devices, generally perceived as incompatible, to create a new narrative. Frank D'Angelo writes that pastiche, like parody, "is a contemporary rhetorical form of borrowing, imitating, and pasting together other forms."[44] However, scholar and Cultural Studies theorist Frederic Jameson, specifically distinguishes pastiche from parody. The former tends to not be political as it lacks "parody's ulterior motives, amputated of the satiric impulse, devoid of laughter."[45] This particular statement can be debated depending on the text because some pastiche narratives disguise their politics and ideology in various ways. Nevertheless, it serves as an important reminder to the reader to observe if a particular pastiche is more about recycling aesthetic pleasure rather than ideological deconstruction.

Linda Hutcheon is one of the important critics who addresses the preoccupation (as stated by Jameson) of scholars with the political intent of self-reflexive postmodern narratives. She writes, "Modeling postmodernism as a general cultural enterprise from postmodern architecture, I would have to argue that it is both and neither: it sits on the fence between a need (often ironic) to recall the past of our lived cultural environment and a desire (often ironized too) to change its present."[46] This conceptualization is closer to what Los Bros employ in their narratives than Jameson's views.

Gilbert's "BEM" functions as a pastiche in Hutcheon's terms because it is a Hispanic/Latino noirish/science fiction/comic adventure that mixes genres and, while maintaining a serious tone, manages to imbue the narrative with some dark humor, yet appears to parody certain elements of repetition in serial adventures while also empowering the Latina characters. Meanwhile Jaime's "Mechan-X" presents a more low-key storytelling, in which the reader is introduced to another bizarre genre mix that features the comedic sci-fi misadventures of Maggie, and her crush on intergalactic hero Rand Race. The setting of this story is in the future, but it feels more like a contemporary romantic comedy adventure than the often gloomy asexual worlds of science fiction. However, like Gilbert, Jaime empowers his Latina characters by parodying the absurdity of science fiction comics and the overly masculine heroes promoted by the American comic book industry.

Gilbert's "BEM" was originally published in a shorter version and later expanded into five separate segments that were included in the premiere issue of *Love and Rockets* published by Fantagraphics. Nowadays, most readers experience the story in its entirety in the collection *Amor y Cohetes*, which compiles random pieces published by Los Bros in the magazine, stories not linked by continuity to the *Palomar* and *Locas* sagas. This particular piece is very difficult to read at first because Gilbert takes a novelistic approach with his short story and introduces a variety of points of view in the narrative, while meshing visuals from detective noir and monster films with the tropical setting of a fictional Latin American country. It takes several readings and paying close attention to the plot to figure out all the character chess pieces he is setting up and how their roles pay off at the end with his deconstruction of repetitive genre adventures. BEM himself, the main antagonist character,

Luba, Roxanne, and Patrice use different types of dance to seduce the monster. Gilbert Hernandez, *Amor y Cohetes*, 28. © Gilbert Hernandez.

remains a complete mystery for most of the story, and we only hear about him through other characters who have their own agendas.

The first couple of pages show a series of fast transitions that, while connected thematically, introduce a variety of points of view to present the multiple voices of the story. First, we are introduced to a giant insect-like monster approaching an island.[47] This creature seems like a retro homage to the monster movies that Los Bros used to enjoy as children in the 1950s and 1960s. The action visually shifts to an apartment, where the distraught character of Leonore is introduced.[48] Her boyfriend connects this setting to the plot as he tries to comfort her, explaining that the monster will not kill people because the government is evacuating the island. Leonore is in a state of shock because she has been dreaming about BEM, another menace and the villain of the piece. The action then shifts to another apartment, where a news anchorman is explaining that BEM is a dangerous escaped criminal.[49] An unknown female viewer in the room is horrified at the news while being stalked in the background by a monstrous arm that the reader might suspect is BEM. The setting shifts to another apartment, where we are introduced to a mysterious male figure preparing to fight BEM while looking at a picture of a former lover.[50] This visual juxtaposition of the threat of a woman with a hero who is attempting to avenge a former lover finally gives the reader something palpable: the typical antagonistic setting of a serial adventure.

The whole introduction, however, is disorienting and creates a disjointed

Luba escapes the narrative loop by becoming a revolutionary, while Radium continues to jump buildings. Gilbert Hernandez, *Amor y Cohetes*, 48. © Gilbert Hernandez.

narrative, as each action features a different set of characters and only lasts for a few panels, connected with scene-to-scene transitions. This is a narrative device that Gilbert will develop further in the *Palomar* stories.

The setup is expanded when Gilbert introduces an earlier non-canonical version of Luba and Peter Río, the protagonist couple of *Poison River*.[51] Luba is presented as the typical sexualized figure of Latino musicals or adventure magazines, and she plans to seduce and control the monster (bizarrely with her sensuality) with the intentions of acquiring power. Later, the readers are presented with Roxanne, another sexy female character, who, along with her friend Paulo, is also trying to seduce the giant insect beast by using a Latin beat.[52] Finally, Patrice, a classical ballet dancer, offers a third take on what type of music and dance must be used to seduce the monster.

This particular employment of Latin culture and sexuality is interesting

Subverting the Intertextual Comic Book Corporate Structure

because it rarely appears in this type of fantasy/science fiction setting, and here it serves as a parody of the notion of stereotypical Latin sensuality that used to pervade old-fashioned American musicals. This is probably the earliest time in Gilbert's narrative where one can identify his whimsical but bizarre portrayal of sexuality that some readers find offensive. Some could find the drawings of Luba to be exploitative of the female body, but to me the outrageous visual juxtaposition of the monster with the sexualized female character serves rather as an ironic depiction of that exploitation. This is particularly relevant in view of the history of stereotypical exposure of the female body in musicals featuring Latina characters.

At this point in the narrative the reader may be confused because there is no clear protagonist or genre markings in the story. Gilbert had previously introduced the hard-boiled character of detective Radium (the mysterious male figure preparing to fight BEM at the very beginning), who seems to be the hero of the story. However, the detective's quest ends in failure when he realizes that the BEM he defeated was a decoy criminal brainwashed by the real BEM.[53] This is a turning point in the narrative, which leaves the reader confused and intrigued by the juxtaposition of the ridiculous monster story, exotic Latin musical tropes, and the gritty and noirish pursuit of BEM.

The two storylines (the monster attacking the island and Detective Radium's preparation to fight BEM) finally come together when, after Luba and Roxanne fail to seduce the monster with their feminine guiles, it/he reveals that it/he actually has intelligence. This development is revealed to be a plot designed by the mysterious BEM, who was experimenting on the monster but was unable to complete these experiments because he was imprisoned. The monster story is concluded with new revelations that provide the climactic deconstructionist statement of the story.

As mentioned earlier, Russian critic Bakhtin used the metaphor of the carnival to explain the idea of heteroglossia, because carnival is the social event where multiple voices meet, coexist, and clash. The last part of "BEM" takes place precisely at a carnival celebrated in the fictional place of San Sassafras. Despite the fact that Gilbert was probably unfamiliar with Bakhtin's work, his story fits perfectly into the Russian critic's theoretical conceptualizations. All of the random characters and their individual points of view finally meet at the carnival, and an explanation of what is happening is provided.[54] In this celebration, everyone is inebriated and lustful and the streets are overrun with drunks and orgies. The monster arrives and indulges in the lowest basic instincts of humanity until he confronts the characters of Luba, Radium, and Beatrice.

Shifting genres. Jaime Hernandez, *Maggie the Mechanic*, 7. © Jamie Hernandez.

After the battle, Beatrice, a character with telepathic powers, explains to her boyfriend (and the audience) that BEM had killed detective Radium after escaping from prison and had taken his form to flee the authorities. He had suffered brain damage in the process, and as a result was trapped mimicking the figure of the detective rather than his own identity. BEM's subconscious had called the insect-like monster to help him recover his identity, but that monster is killed by Radium/BEM before it could provide any assistance. Beatrice remarks that now BEM is trapped in the perfect prison (Radium's body and his quest to eradicate a BEM), an ironic situation, as Radium *is* BEM.[55] This creates an endless and unfulfillable quest that mocks the repetitive loops in serial adventures where the hero is constantly chasing after one villain, yet they need each other to continue existing. The end of the story includes a

Subverting the Intertextual Comic Book Corporate Structure

minor political aspect, because while the traditional hero/antagonist Radium/BEM continues to chase himself/itself in an artificial unfulfilling quest, Luba is able to escape the narrative loop and gain political prominence as a result of these events. The narration indicates she would evolve ideologically and become a revolutionary, while Radium would continue to jump buildings in his search for BEM.[56]

The story is a serious parody, where the characters come from different genre traditions. The narrative is exciting and quite serious in tone, and it is obvious that Gilbert is well familiar with all the genres he is bringing together. While the fictional Latin American setting may confuse the reader a little, it is the ambiguities in the construction of BEM as a character that affect how we perceive the entire cast. We are not sure about the intentions of the characters and their specific relationship with BEM, something that superhero narratives tend to avoid in their clear distinction between good and evil, and between protagonist and secondary characters.

Jaime Hernandez's "Mechan-X" is different from "BEM." It introduces the characters of Maggie and Hopey, two of the main protagonists in the *Locas* saga, but follows Maggie's point of view. The first page shows them struggling to wake up in their apartment after having partied until very late, and there are many visual elements that immediately stand out. Both female characters are drawn to appear in their twenties; their apartment is messy and unkempt. Both are shown as having slept together on the same sofa, and Hopey is shirtless and showing her breasts. However, it is uncertain whether they are in a romantic lesbian relationship, because no sex is actually shown, and their behavior could be interpreted as common in urban housemates from the "punk" era. Furthermore, it is unclear whether the characters are Hispanic because of the absence of "traditional" ethnic signifiers such as the use of Spanish interspersed with their English.

This somewhat realistic depiction of ordinary life, in which Maggie complains about her unstable career, is disrupted in the last drawing of the sequence where Maggie is drawn riding a sci-fi hoverbike to work.[57]

After a page composed of sequential drawings in a trashy apartment, Jaime changes the readers' expectations by switching genres within the same page. This strategy continues on the following couple of pages, where the science fiction setting is modified to fit the conventions of a romantic comedy. Maggie falls clumsily from her hoverbike, and she is embarrassingly introduced to her love interest Rand Race, the best mechanic in the universe. In the last drawing of the second page, Jaime introduces Maggie's full name as Margaret Chascarrillo, which could be perceived as an ambivalent Latino presentation that combines an Anglophone first name with a last name usually associated with a Hispanic background.[58] More possible links to Latin culture are introduced in the first sequential drawing of the third page, when Rand Race recognizes that Maggie is the niece of Victoria Chascarrillo, the legendary Latina wrestler.[59]

In the next couple of pages, Jaime infuses this bizarre science fiction narrative with comic relief and the opposite of the sense of epic grandeur that readers often expect from these types of fantasies. Race, who is drawn as the handsome American pulp sci-fi heroes such as Flash Gordon and Buck Rogers, practically tells Maggie that his legendary fame is due to his fixing the limo of H. R. Costigan, one of the most famous millionaires in the galaxy. This confession of Race that downplays his heroism is mixed with Maggie's clumsy actions that serve as a comic relief—for example, when she accidentally sprays her boss with water. The boss' reaction is drawn humorously, like a comedy strip in the style of *Blondie*, an interesting visual juxtaposition with the handsome drawings of Race and Maggie that adhere more to a style usually associated with serious science fiction adventures.[60]

After Rand and his boss blow up the machinery they are fixing because it would take too long to fix, through Maggie's eyes the reader can see the sleazier aspects of Jaime's sci-fi universe.[61] In their travel back to the city, the three characters encounter broken robots and an enemy from Race's past who wants to force them to fix the robots for him. They escape thanks to Maggie, who lives to tell her story to her roommate Hopey and to her friend Penny Century.[62] Another layer of sleaze is added to Rand's depiction when Penny, who has dated him before, reacts strongly to his being Maggie's boss.[63] Rand thus represents male fantasies about an idealized masculinity and its relationship to heroism, a vision debunked by the strong and self-sufficient female characters who see him for what he truly is, an incompetent untrustworthy ordinary man. Jaime's "Mechan-X" stands out with its clumsy and sleazy science fiction world that parodies the ideals of modernity.

The common strand in Gilbert's "BEM" and Jaime's "Mechan-X" is that, through the parody of the genres that dominate the industry, both Latina heroines (Luba and Maggie) become the protagonists, while both Anglophone heroes (Radium and Race, respectively) are portrayed as ineffective in fulfilling the heroic roles they are supposed to represent. This is a vast deviation from the comic book norm, as Latinas are often represented in American culture as a symbol of sexuality or buffoonery, which Luba and Maggie are in certain ways at the beginning of each story. It is obvious that the authors identify with them and that Luba and Maggie represent Gilbert and Jaime's

Shifting the narrative tone through visuals. Jaime Hernandez, *Maggie the Mechanic*, 10. © Jamie Hernandez.

outsider status in relation to hegemony. Through the parody of the masculine Anglophone heroes, the Latina characters become more attractive to the readers, which will set up their next adventures in the *Palomar* and *Locas* sagas.

As I hope this explanation shows, both Gilbert and Jaime's stories in the first issue of *Love and Rockets* are complex postmodern pastiches where the comic book reader needs to be familiar with the tropes that the two brothers are appropriating from previous comics and other types of popular culture to create entertaining narratives that serve as parodies of the mediums at the time but that certainly injected a new energy to the alternative scene in the comic book industry of the United States. This postmodern storytelling would be later used in their *Palomar* and *Locas* sagas in which the constant clash of comic genres represents the Bakhtinian dialogism or confrontation of characters' perspectives. Next, I will focus on Penny Century, a secondary character of the *Locas* saga whose storyline best represents Los Bros' relationship with the comic book industry's main source of intertextuality: the American superhero.

Jaime's *Penny Century* Saga: Its Homage and Derision of the Superhero Genre

As previously discussed, superhero comics have been parodied and critiqued since the 1950s (Harvey Kutzman's *Mad* and others), and astute observations about the genre certainly helped foment the deconstructionist superhero movement from the 1980s, spearheaded by the likes of Frank Miller with his *Batman* and *Daredevil* runs and Alan Moore with his *Watchmen* miniseries. This new type of self-reflexive and self-referential comic book storytelling works better with an audience that understands its hidden references, and it certainly thrived in the last couple of decades with the rise of the direct market and its faithful fan culture.

In recent times, superhero intertextual narratives have been well-written and fun but controversial, because writers in independent comic companies are often able to dodge the limitations imposed by mainstream companies and their corporate affiliates and write storylines where the characters mimic their mainstream counterparts, while portraying the violence in a more realistic manner and at times amplifying the political nature of the text. The character of Superman is a good case in point. Among the most recent critically acclaimed metaversions of Superman are Mark Millar's *Superman: Red Son*, Mark Waid's *Irredeemable*, and Robert Kirkman's *Invincible*. These comics feature heroes that resemble Marvel and DC Comics characters, with staples such as Superman providing a textual reference for the new characters and rooting the reader in something they already know.

The parodies function in different manners. Mark Millar's *Red* Son is an official Superman adaptation where the writer created a story in which Superman fell in the Soviet Union instead of the United States when he first arrived on Earth. Because Millar has permission from DC Comics, the copyright owners, he was able to transform the story and twist the ideological background of the character but was able to use the same DC Comics characters that many readers from around the world would recognize, such as Batman, Lois Lane, and Lex Luthor. In contrast, in *Irredeemable*, Mark Waid created the Plutonian, a fictional character that resembles Superman and shares many of his plotlines. The character was published by BOOM, outside of DC Comics, so Waid uses appropriation techniques to create a twisted visual echo of the "Superman" story in which the Plutonian (Superman's parody/homage) becomes a rogue that destroys most of the cities in the world. Robert Kirkman's *Invincible* in turn is more of a pastiche because its intertextuality is less focused on DC's narrative, and its young protagonist Invincible draws material from and pays homage to several characters and publishing brands simultaneously.

The problem with these intertextual narratives is that the deconstruction they offer is often superficial and is still designed primarily to provide entertainment relying on large-scale battles and exploitative sensuality. Many superhero readers enjoy them because they see these comics as an evolution in the genre, and because through these narratives they are able to justify reading what mainstream society considers too silly for adults. Marvel and DC Comics have recognized the need to feed these "mature" intertextual narratives to their consumers, so even the big companies that were initially parodied have tried to mine economically this self-referential business. For example, in 2000, Marvel unleashed their Ultimate Universe, in which their characters got a contemporary and more realistic spin. Marvel kept publishing the original version of the characters that fulfilled their family-friendly vision, while the Ultimate Universe provided a more cynical, experimental, and political storytelling. However, the ability of Marvel and DC to assimilate this type of storytelling raises the question whether these intertextual narratives are subversive enough to move away from the genre or whether they are simply opportunistic imitations that exploit properties owned by corporations.

One of the most influential comic book writers that has used intertextuality to first parody the genre and its market and then transcend its confinements is Alan Moore. His earlier work such as *Watchmen* displays self-awareness about the role of adventure comics as teenagers' fantasies with the inclusion of the pirate adventure strip that is situated inside the story while playing a role in the main apocalyptic plot. Once working outside the confines of Marvel and DC, Moore was able to explore ideas and subtexts of comic art and the superhero language in more depth in his opus *Promethea* (drawn by J. H. Williams). Here, the structure of the narrative was not conceived to just entertain older superhero readers in an adult but straightforward narrative but to debate the role of the author, the reader, and the genre.

Similarly to Alan Moore in his later work, the Hernandez Brothers do not aim to improve the superhero narrative but instead use it as just one of many building blocks in the creation of original auteur stories. Jaime's Penny Century character is a case in point, because her superhero narrative is not the main focus of the *Locas* storyline and is not targeted to superhero readers. Penny is an important character, but her superhero fantasies are a subplot among many important ones in Jaime's *Locas* universe. Jaime's specific references and narrative devices clearly show he is familiar with superhero narratives, but they are not designed to poach and profit commercially from the mainstream narratives. Penny serves in the saga simply as a link to a "super-

Linking fantasy and reality through lettering. Jaime Hernandez, *Maggie the Mechanic*, 23. © Jamie Hernandez.

hero language" of the American comic book industry that would be familiar to wider comic book audiences.

Penny Century's first appearance was in the first issue of *Love and Rockets* in the one-page story "Penny Century, You're Fired!," which features jarring shifts in space, time, and reality.[64]

The first drawing shows Penny seeing herself as Atoma, an invincible superheroine. It is obvious that she is imagining this because we see the superheroic visuals in a comic cloud over her head. The next image interrupts the daydreaming, as we see Penny's manager slapping her and firing her from the factory where she works. Jaime uses the lettering to tie together dream and abrupt awakening when Penny says in her fantasy, "Little do they know that in reality I am . . . ," a sentence completed by the manager, who announces that her civilian identity is being fired. The next drawings in the one-page se-

Subverting the Intertextual Comic Book Corporate Structure

Maggie's disappointment with the superhero as a model of masculinity. Jaime Hernandez, *Maggie the Mechanic*, 93. © Jamie Hernandez.

quence also disrupt time and space, as they present a glamorous Penny flirting with Costigan, a millionaire with two horns on his head. The shift in setting also changes the genre from a worker narrative to a bourgeois melodrama, in which Costigan is offering everything to Penny in exchange for her love. She tells him that the only thing she wants from him is his help in turning her into a superpowered heroine. He responds in a melodramatic manner that this is the only thing he cannot give her, to the disappointment of Penny, who ends the story by watching superheroes flying in the city and wistfully admitting, "I knew it was too good to be true." This one-page story is very provocative in terms of the comic book industry because female characters and the female audience have been consistently ignored by the mainstream comic book companies. Penny's fantasies then serve almost as a plea to allow women into these masculine narratives and a market that has been clearly defined in masculine terms.

A few issues further into the *Love and Rockets* run, Jaime continues to mock masculine superheroes in his story "Maggie vs. Maniakk." In this parody of the superhero genre, Maggie recounts to her girlfriends (which include superhero wannabe Penny Century) how she flirted with the idea of being a superhero. One day, she accidentally freed a supervillain from a dimensional prison that had been set up by a superhero.[65] Maggie researches the plot in her old comics, finds out that Ultimax had previously defeated Maniakk, and enlists the help of that superhero in her quest to recapture Maniakk. Maggie complains about the subpar art in Ultimax's comic and is shocked to discover that the superhero had sold his mansion and is now a deadbeat who lives in the worst part of town.[66] Through this narrative development, Jaime is debunking the close association of the American male superhero with the dominant sectors of the American economy. The first visual depiction of Ultimax is that of an unkempt character who lives with a group of drunks in a filthy apartment with cracked walls.[67] This representation is reminiscent of Kurtzman's "Superduperman" parody, in which the female characters are utterly disappointed with the masculine superhero's violent needs and unbridled sexuality.

Ultimax puts himself back in shape with a potion as soon as he hears Maggie's story about his nemesis. He asks her to be his sidekick go-go girl, a demeaning position that involves nothing more than Maggie's being pretty.[68] The previous go-go girl had become Demona, the most powerful heroine in the world, and could no longer put up with Ultimax's misogynistic behavior. Once Ultimax appears again in public, Maggie regrets having been involved in the plot because she finds unleashing the hero unto society more annoying than liberating the villain. At the end, the superhero and the supervillain beat each other to a pulp, and it is obvious that their antagonism has not led anywhere. Kurtzman's "Superduperman" similarly ends with the two protagonists beating each other to a pulp and a disappointed Lois Lane standing by.[69]

At the end of the story, Penny Century reacts badly to Maggie's account because she is jealous that Maggie became involved in a superhero plot, even if only in an obvious mockery of the genre's function as a masculine fantasy. Penny had tried to acquire superpowers in previous issues and even had visited Maggie in the jungle to see if the native tribe there could give her "magical" instead of industrial power.[70] She continually fails to become a superheroine, and this string of failures becomes one of the subplots of the *Locas* saga.

The facade of the "blonde bombshell with superhero ambitions" develops in an interesting manner throughout the *Locas* saga. As the story progresses and Jaime diminishes the supernatural and fantasy content in the storyline, Penny's plot gradually becomes similar to a soap opera, in which a poor girl (Penny) marries an aristocrat (Costigan) and has to learn how to deal with her ascent to the upper classes and her new role as the mother of Negra. When Maggie and her friends visit her, Penny is throwing outlandish parties and participating in re-creations of her superheroic fantasies, as her new economic status has not fulfilled her and she is still focused on achieving the idyllic idea of the superhero. It is revealed later through a series of flashbacks in the story "Bay of Threes" how miserable Penny was when she was a poor girl called Beatriz García. When she discovers comic books in high school, she sees an outlet that would help her escape her reality, a development reminiscent of Cervantes's *Don Quixote*, whose protagonist was able to escape from his drudgery through chivalry books.[71]

In contrast to *Don Quixote*, which refers to particular earlier texts, however, Jaime's parody does not reference directly other comics or ideas, as he is not interested in improving/parodying the visual vocabulary of the DC and Marvel superhero narratives.[72] He situates the genre archetypes and references within his own authorial universe, a sort of "Jaime intertextuality." Due to this choice, the readers participate in a complex self-referential work that is related specifically to the *Love and Rockets* universe, and they do not need to understand a complex continuity or archetypes built by the mainstream corporations in order to see the meaning of the story.[73]

Jaime later began to shift the *Locas* saga into a superhero yarn itself, full of complex continuities and almost returning to the fantasy elements of its first segments. The seeds of the story were planted (toward the end of the second volume) when Maggie lives in an L.A. apartment complex where she also works as the superintendent and finds out that one of the tenants (Alarma Kraktovilova) in the complex is a Russian American superheroine.[74] This seemingly minute detail becomes surprisingly significant later, in the third volume, when the superhero reality/plotline is reprised.

Penny Century breaks the rules in order to acquire superpowers. Jaime Hernandez, *God and Science: The Return of the Ti-Girls*, 17. © Jamie Hernandez.

As part of the relaunch of the *Love and Rockets* anthology, Jaime published the superheroine storyline "The Return of the Ti-Girls" in the first two issues, which functioned as a complex, *Locas*-continuity-laden storyline but also as a beautiful closure to the *Penny Century* plotline.[75] The story was later reprinted as a graphic novel (*God and Science: The Return of the Ti-Girls*) with additional pages, and it follows the adventures of the Ti-Girls and their struggles to stop a Penny Century who had become insane in the process of gaining superpowers. This story could be confusing to newer *Locas* fans because it serves as a metaphor of Penny's life, yet is still linked to the main

Locas plot because it features Maggie as herself and living in her reality. In addition, many of the superheroines are played by different female characters that had previously appeared in Jaime's work, which gives an additional intertextual pleasure to the *Love and Rockets* reader yet can be a little daunting to someone who is reading this book as a standalone text.[76] Ironically, even though there are no references to companies such as Marvel and DC, because of the self-referentiality of "The Return of the Ti-Girls," reading this text can be as overwhelming a task as trying to fully understand all the characters and their backgrounds in a recent issue of the *X-Men* or *Batman* series.

For example, there are several intertextual allusions to past *Locas* characters that were clear to me because I recently reread all of Jaime's work over the course of several weeks and therefore I could identify some of the important references he made to his own work and how he retrofitted them in "The Return of the Ti-Girls." For example, an intertextual reference to Jaime's work is his depiction of Xochimitl (Maggie's cousin), who appears as one of the venerable older superheroines who are part of the Ti-Girls. Xochimitl's superhero persona parallels her representation in earlier stories where she appeared as a sympathetic professional wrestler. She is not very good at being a superheroine or a wrestler, but she is an empathic character whom everybody admires. More obscure characters from Jaime's other smaller storylines who did not appear in the *Locas* saga, like the robot Cheetah Torpeda, are included in the story for the first time to interact with Maggie and her superheroine versions of the *Locas* cast.

"The Return of the Ti-Girls" was originally printed in the first two issues of the third volume of *Love and Rockets*. The anthology is published annually, a schedule that is likely to affect the reader's original impression of "The Return of the Ti-Girls," as he/she would be unaware of the direction Jaime aims to take with the story. The story begins with a number of slapstick scenes in which Maggie's roommate Angel tries hard to become a superheroine and follow Atoma, who is part of the Fenomenons, the greatest female superheroine team of all time.[77] The superhero plot accelerates when Atoma reveals to Angel that her team is currently hunting Penny Century, who has become dangerous after finally having acquired her powers through illegal means.[78] The now-detached head of the robot character of Cheetah Torpeda (from Jaime's "Rocky and Her Robot" stories) tells Atoma and Angel how Penny accomplished her goal. This revelation is in the form of a long-winded narrative exposition in which we discover how Penny sold an unborn child to a witch named Vakka in exchange for finally gaining superpowers.[79] The exaggerated and melodramatic plotline serves as a metaphor for all the bad

Under Maggie's guidance, Angel discovers the Ti-Girls' adventures in the back of the comic book store. Jaime Hernandez, *God and Science: The Return of the Ti-Girls*, 12. © Jamie Hernandez.

decisions that Penny Century has made in her life, especially her guilt about difficult choices she had to make previously about motherhood, a topic barely discussed in mainstream superhero adventures.

The art used for the flashback sequence is a clear visual indication of the subversion of the superhero genre. Each of the four panels in which Penny is granted and first enjoys her superpowers also features prominently her toddler Maite. As mother and daughter acquire superhero powers together, they immediately don costumes complete with capes and the initials P and M, respectively, and their first act as superheroines is to fly. However, instead of supporting society's progress, they do mischief, including damaging a giant poster advertising the comic books of their rival superheroine, Cheetah Torpeda. By granting Maite superpowers, Penny, a Latina character, opens the door for the next generation's access to the Establishment. More importantly, she subverts the established order in which superheroes represent white hegemony. In addition, as always in Jaime's art, there is a sharp contrast between

    Subverting the Intertextual Comic Book Corporate Structure

the black and white objects in the panels (for example, Penny's hair and her costume, or her nudity and the shadow of the witch in the background), which further underscores the gap between a typical superhero narrative and the story of *Penny Century*. Even more so, this gap can be seen in the contrast between the high energy and disruptiveness of the art and Cheetah's narration, displayed as monotonous text boxes at the top of each panel and consisting of equal number of lines in adjacent panels. Cheetah, the institutional superheroine, attempts to control the narrative but cannot, as the drawings are much more lively and interesting than her narration.

Interestingly, Maggie explains superhero realities to Angel through her comic book knowledge, thus making sense of the rules and structure of the genre to the comic book reader as well. She takes Angel to the comic book store, points out the overabundance of the elitist Anglophone superhero titles on the stands (mentioning the Fenomenons as an example), and leads her to obscure titles in the hidden back-issue comics, where she learns more about the underdog team named the Ti-Girls.[80]

This particular segment is a self-reflexive statement about the direct-market comic book stores' retail space, which displays the product of the hegemonic companies in a prominent place (as explained in my introduction) and pushes back the most interesting diverse superhero narratives, which are not necessarily successful with customers but feature more compelling characters. It also sets up the explanation of why Penny Century's quest to become a heroine is not just a whim, as she represents the less prominent ethnic groups in the American comic book industry.

Jaime's final storyline can seem strange even to a *Locas* fan, as its melodramatic plot abounds in absurd themes and twists that belong to outdated superhero comic books from the 1960s. A contemporary superhero reader would be disappointed because the author is not commenting intertextually on the superhero comics published today, and some of the *Love and Rockets* readers may find the aesthetics too goofy, old-fashioned, and nostalgic in comparison with some of the more experimental work Jaime has previously done in the anthology. The reason the story works, however, is precisely because of its outdated qualities. First, this retro/nostalgic style Jaime uses follows more closely the superhero comics he read as a child, and second, the character of Penny Century is more likely to see herself involved in an adventure that resembled the comics from her own childhood.

At some point in "The Return of the Ti-Girls," Penny loses her powers and her memories as punishment for her irresponsible deeds, but it is some-

Penny Century turns the superhero world on its head. Jaime Hernandez, *God and Science: The Return of the Ti-Girls*, 73. © Jamie Hernandez.

thing that, according to Jaime's story, happens to every superheroine as she moves on with her life.[81] Penny finds new meaning in her role as a mother in her amnesia, but not without having changed the elitist superheroine infrastructure through her resistance to conformity and her exclusion. In a particular line she echoes Jaime's vision when she says, "Before all this, I wanted so bad to be invited to the party, but now I find it far more fun to be the party crasher. I mean look at me! I am having the best time!"[82]

As this image shows, Penny has literally turned the superhero world on its head. There is a sharp contrast between hers and Angel's worlds underscored by the monochrome drawings. Penny takes up the entire left half of the frame, and her world, a starry sky at the top of the panel, presses down on a disgruntled Angel, who is center frame yet blends into the white background. More importantly, Maggie peeks out at the other two characters from the bottom right corner of the panel, clearly enjoying Penny's words. As a reader,

Subverting the Intertextual Comic Book Corporate Structure

As an experienced comic book reader, Maggie is able to make sense of Penny Century's story. Jaime Hernandez, *God and Science: The Return of the Ti-Girls*, 128. © Jamie Hernandez.

she is content to see a different type of superheroine, one who is pushing the narrative in a new direction.

All the characters who have come into contact with Penny are fundamentally affected by her. In the quest to stop Penny Century, characters such as the Russian Atoma change their allegiance from the elitist superhero group to the more grounded and likable Ti-Girls. Others such as the portly Angel get to experience a heroic adventure before they move on with their lives. Therefore, Penny's quest at heart has opened up the language of superhero comics, something that is essential in a good parody. Still, I would argue that the main difference is that the intertextuality used by Jaime serves the purpose of redeeming the defiance of alternative comics rather than solidifying the discourse of corporate mainstream superheroes.[83]

The role of Maggie as a Latina comic book reader is central to the story because she is the one who is able to decode the imagery, characters, and plots of what is happening to her and her friends. In a self-reflexive device, toward the end of the story she interacts with the superhero characters, and her comic book knowledge allows her to figure out Jaime's otherwise incoherent plot. Maggie tells the superheroines that she has drawn the information from the comics, which they themselves cannot read, since the pages look blank to them. Maggie achieves the transcendental moment of the story when she eventually figures out that Penny has always had her superpowers (something important for a female Latina), and that her complexes and desires to be part of the superhero game were what stunted her abilities.[84] Maggie cries when Penny forgets about her adventures, especially since she realizes that Penny has always belonged in the superhero genre and not in more realistic comics, a realization triggered by the fact that Penny never grows old. She is happy for Penny, as the latter stayed into the idealized superhero reality, while Maggie herself goes back to her "alternative comics" reality (as one of the characters tells her, "True, but in this particular scenario it is you who is not regular flesh and blood").[85] Maggie remarks ironically to the superheroine characters that helped Penny: "See you in the funny papers," before fading out and leaving them on a blank page with no background and nothing to talk about.[86] In this case, Maggie as the reader is the authority figure (not the author) whose fandom and knowledge is what gives meaning to the text and solves the puzzle.

In this chapter, my main goal was to explain how parody functions as an intertextual technique and produces ambivalence of meaning. I also aimed to apply the theory of intertextuality to Los Bros' works in an accessible manner and to explain the importance of this theoretical concept in understanding the postmodern aspects of their stories. Even though their role as authors is important in order to understand the context of their narratives, they themselves acknowledge, specifically in Jaime's *Penny Century* adventures, that the reader himself/herself is the key to understanding the text. In the next chapter, I will explore further how the Latino signifiers and cultural content of the story may or may not affect the process of reading and decodifying in the story.

Robots in Jaime's "Rocky" Stories and Gilbert's *Citizen Rex*

ROBOTS ARE A staple of comic book culture that can be traced all the way back to Golden Age serials such as *Buck Rogers* and remain relevant in current sci-fi and superhero adventures. I already mentioned Maggie and Rand Race's encounter with robots in Jaime's "Mechan-X" in order to demonstrate how the author manipulated certain genre archetypes. These robots were visualized as trash in a junkyard, and by representing them as garbage, Jaime parodied the technological fetishes of genre comics. While both Jaime and Gilbert have used robots in their stories to replicate or subvert certain science fiction conventions, they have also tackled political ideas that are intrinsic to robot narratives and that often appear in ethnic narratives as well.

Throughout their evolution in science fiction literature, robots have been used to represent various aspects of humanity. These include, but are not limited to, serving as metaphors of the workers' struggle in Karl Capek's *R.U.R.*, embodying a superior rationalism in Isaac Asimov's *I, Robot*, and exemplifying the sinister machinations of modernity in James Cameron's *Terminator* films. Robot stories can be easily adapted to any contemporary issue, as they tend to be used as a metaphor for the best and worst that humanity has to offer. More recently, with films such as *A.I.: Artificial Intelligence* and

WALL-E, the robot genre has begun to employ narrative tropes related to ecology in order to tackle topical issues about how humanity relates to nature.

Jaime's "Rocky" stories are about Rocky's growing into an adult and her coming to terms with being raised in a small town. The setting itself is strange to science fiction, as this genre rarely features small-town coming-of-age stories. Rocky and her robot Fumble share down-to-earth adventures that revolve predominantly around Rocky's melodramatic relationship with her parents instead of the epic plots usually associated with science fiction. This bucolic utopia ends with the last story, "Rocky's Birthday Surprise," in which Rocky visits her sister in the big city. After running into a black hole, Rocky and her robot are transported to another planet, Bako Mato, a place where politics and ideology are finally introduced into the storyline. Rocky is unable to handle the new situation or to prevail over local villain Rongo Ragney, who wants to destroy all robots. Rescued by the robot heroine Cheetah Torpeda, she makes it home safe, but ends up stranded back on the planet for over twelve years after the robot Fumble pleads with her to return and help the robots' cause.[1] Rocky reappears briefly in the story "Rocky in Rocket Rhodes," where she reveals that she, unfortunately, has lost contact with Fumble and Cheetah Torpeda. Rocky's journey is very similar to Maggie's, as both characters are interested above all in their melodramatic relationships and lose contact with friends who are more concerned with revolutionary ideology.

In the most recent Hernandez Brothers' robot story, *Citizen Rex*, Gilbert and Mario attempt to construct a Latin American dystopian science fiction in which the plot and the characters are centered on the mysterious robot Rex, a narrative technique very similar to Gilbert's use of the antagonist BEM in his original story "BEM." Rex almost fulfills Asimov's ideals about robots because he is an antihero that defies all types of human authorities (aristocracy, mobsters, government, army, and corporations) on his quest to improve humankind. This science fiction comic has some interesting social topics but it does not always play to Gilbert's strengths as an artist because, as Gilbert himself has acknowledged, he cannot draw cars or city landscapes very well. His action scenes are thus clumsy in comparison to those of other comic book artists, and Mario's screenplay provides a scattered plot that is difficult to follow.

Despite its flaws, *Citizen Rex* is very original in how it deals with racial hybridity, especially in a Latin American setting. Latin American intellectuals often embrace the idea of racial *mestizaje* in order to criticize the United

States' racial stratification. Gilbert and Mario poke fun at this idea, as in the story many characters of presumably Latin American origin hate the concept of half-human, half-robot cyborgs. The metaphorical hybridization of robots parodies American fears of miscegenation but also ridicules the presumed racial enlightenment of Latinos, who would fear acquiring a new hybrid identity, too.

chapter two

The Revision of Latino Experience through Comic Book Genres and Soap Opera Devices in Gilbert's *Palomar* and Jaime's *Locas* Sagas

AS STATED IN the introduction of this book, Gilbert's *Palomar* and Jaime's *Locas* sagas are some of the most complex storylines to appear in the American comic book industry due to their thematic intricacy, multiple volumes, and long period of publication that has spanned over thirty years. This type of narrative requires a lot of commitment on the part of the reader, yet is something normal for experienced comic book fans who are accustomed to collecting comics and to reading endless pages of serialized storylines about the characters they follow. Traditional audiences, in contrast, tend to expect shorter narratives with a clear beginning and end. In the first chapter, I discussed how Los Bros Hernandez's narratives contain complex intertextual elements that range from insider knowledge of the American comic book industry to the aesthetic allusions and parodies of certain genres enjoyed by traditional comic book readers. Jaime and Gilbert add another layer of complexity by also having ethnic signifiers embedded into their narratives due to their Latino/Mexican American/Chicano heritage. I argued that some of the Latino elements may be difficult to decode, even for Hispanic readers (for example, if they are not familiar with West Coast Mexican American experience), but that they remain very important in their role in the parodic depiction of Anglophone genres such as science fiction and superheroes.

In this chapter, I explore the visualization of the "ethnic Latino" factor of this complex intertextuality in Gilbert's *Palomar* and Jaime's *Locas* story-lines. While both artists play with genres that are popular in the American comic book industry, and others that are more relevant to their Latino/ Mexican American heritage, both creators express several important ideas about the political evolution of Latino ethnic identity, while using sexuality and gender tropes to engage the reader with a subversion of both American and Mexican/Latino genres that disrupt utopian and traditional Anglophone and Latino paradigms.[1]

Up until the recent stories in 2014, Gilbert's *Palomar* universe has presented the story of two types of Latino experiences in the United States. Gilbert depicts the life of immigrants (Luba and some of her relatives) who have moved from their original indeterminate Latin American national space into a new reality in the United States. Further, he has developed Latino characters (for example, Venus and Fritz) who are born in the United States and whose identity struggles play a different role in the narrative. As some of the immigrant characters in Gilbert's saga (such as Pipo) gain economic wealth and enter the film industry over the course of the story, they begin to re-create their experiences through B movies (in the form of original graphic novels) that clearly do not retell the story as previously written.

Gilbert playfully parodies the unreliability of the ethnic narrative and how reality is subjective to the author's desires and the readers' awareness. However, this approach is not intended to criticize ethnic narratives but rather to glorify them. First, Gilbert establishes the contradictions between the "intellectual" narrative that often fails to completely interact with the subaltern it aims to represent on the one hand and the mass culture that serves to provide hegemonic control but actually reaches the masses on the other. I intend to show how Gilbert, through Fritz's movies/graphic novels, displays the contemporary postmodern view, namely, that when minority groups feel comfortable enough to manipulate their own story, a sense of empowerment is revealed, a move away from their humble beginnings in which they originally could not control the way they were represented.

In Jaime's *Locas* saga, the protagonists Maggie and Hopey are native Latinas, one Chicana and the other of mixed Irish and Colombian heritage, respectively. This particular series takes place predominantly in the United States, and it revolves around the development of the characters into adulthood and their relationships with various members of their community out-side of their Latino friends and family. Even though this is a coming-of-age story, Jaime provides abrupt genre shifts from science fiction and fantasy to realism and back that can be jarring, as its genre self-referentiality is disruptive of the idea of a straightforward narrative.

While his depiction of Maggie's life is mostly linked to narrative genres that the character (and the author) personally enjoys, these genres represent both her Anglo (science fiction, superheroes) and Latino (wrestling) heritages, and the characters embodied by them, Penny Century and Rena Titañón, respectively, visually represent the issues she has with each ethnic culture. Maggie projects a bicultural reality that, while obviously manipulated by Jaime to represent hers and other characters' psyche, visually constructs the life of these Latino, punk, and bisexual characters outside of the rules of both the hegemonic American comic book industry and the canonical ethnic literary parameters.

Both Gilbert and Jaime employ the use of familiar and obscure comic book genres from the two sides of the border to establish a bicultural depiction of Latino life that fits literary devices of the Hispanic/Latino traditions but is also compatible with material previously published in the American comic book industry. I will discuss in detail how this simultaneous compatibility and disruption could be controversial due to the fact that ethnic narratives, the product of a segregated society, used to be perceived as contentious in nature, especially when they aimed to challenge hegemony. I argue that both Jaime's and Gilbert's works are political, but their protagonists are not constructed to be traditional literary ideological mouthpieces. They are postmodern ethnic heroes whose self-awareness and ability to manipulate narrative devices are what empower them.

The Evolution of the Chicano/Latino Narrative: Politics and Postnationalism

During most of the twentieth century, Latinos were one of a number of ethnic and subaltern groups whose voice had been suppressed in the United States, and it was very important for them to establish the relevance of the Latino experience in American cultural production. For example, scholars such as Jorge J. E. Gracia are very adamant that Hispanic/Latino culture had to be historicized and approached dialectically to illustrate how Latino ethnic identity was formed by its clash with American hegemony.[2] This approach has been followed by many Latino artists of Mexican, Cuban, Puerto Rican, Colombian, and other Hispanic backgrounds, artists whose narratives presented a historical/political treatment of their particular subaltern experiences.

In the Southwest and West Coast of the United States, it is obvious that Chicano literature (a term that can be considered problematic today due to its original derogatory connotations and placement of the authors outside of American and Mexican spaces) is the most relevant foundational Latino narrative because Mexican Americans are the majority of the Latino population in these regions. This does not mean, however, that the other Latinos in the area do not share some of the same political experiences. Because of the complexity of the Latinos' ethnic makeup, using the term "Chicano" may be outdated as a strategy for mobilizing the underrepresented Hispanic ethnicities, as it points to exclusively Mexican American discourse. Many cultural critics have focused their research predominantly on the Chicano narrative in the past, but this is changing with the current diversification of the Latino experience. For example, when scholar Ramón Saldívar writes, "Chicano narrative should be seen as an active participant in this reconceptualization of American literary discourse. With African American, feminist, and other formerly ignored American discourses," this type of assessment should not be limited to Chicano storytelling and also has to be applied to other Hispanic/Latino ethnicities in the United States, parallel to models of empowerment used by Native Americans and African Americans in the 1960s and 1970s.[3]

The formation and development of Latino identity and culture in the United States has brought certain successful cultural and political reforms, as well as its share of controversies. While the convergence of the experience of multiple Latin American ethnicities under the "Latino" umbrella has served a political purpose to create solidarity, it has also been considered problematic due to the fact that it allows for the merging of different Hispanic subgroups with their own histories and legacies into a monolithic group, which then can be commodified for commercial purposes. This type of dichotomy has been essential in the debates and disagreements about the Latino canon and how academics choose the texts that represent this complex ethnic group.

Scholar Marion Rohrieltner has traced the development of the "Latino" concept from French economist Michel Chevalier's political use of "panlatinidad" to mark what is not Anglophone in the Americas to its application in the 1980s by scholars and sociologists to create solidarity between Hispanic communities in the United States. Rohrieltner specifically mentions the importance of sociologist Felix Padilla and how the coinage of his term "latinismo" established a difference between self-identification and state-ordained labeling. In his book *Latino Ethnic Consciousness*, Padilla specifically constructed his argument based on the alliances between Mexican and Puerto Rican communities in Chicago formed with the purpose of gaining political power. He explains that this type of umbrella term represents how these different groups have achieved ethnic consciousness as a collective, instead of as scattered minority groups, in order to subvert hegemony and acquire more political prominence.[4]

There has been a history of ethno-nationalist trends in the different Hispanic communities that have clashed with the idea of latinismo/pan-latinidad, as discussed by Marissa Lopez in her book *Chicano Nations*.[5] Scholar Jorge J. E. Gracia wrote against resisting the idea of the Latino collective by appealing to the racial *mestizaje* and social hybridity theories that allegedly make Hispanic/Latin American nations different to the United States. According to him, because Latin American cultures already have a mixed heritage, it would be easy for them to "mix" in the same manner in the United States in order to create a powerful Latino community. Gracia writes, "And our reality is one of mestizaje. Of mixing in every possible way. This is why any barriers between subgroups are largely artificial inventions, the product of ideology and nostalgia, and should not be used to discriminate against, or disparage others. The lack of proper recognition of our common identity forces us to choose sides, to identify with one or another, creating not only dissension, but also a sense of alienation and confusion in others and in ourselves."[6]

However, Marion Rohrieltner points out some of the problems with "Latino" as an umbrella term. In the 1990s, the term began to be used by corporations to target a new ethnic consumer group instead of describing a vibrant activist community. Scholar Silvio Torres-Saillant is particularly harsh on the idea of Latino homogenization for several reasons. First, he criticizes the existing white supremacy in Latin America and the fact that "Many colleagues accept too quickly the view that the Spanish-speaking world has a less racialized and more humane understanding of difference among human beings."[7] Furthermore, according to him, this racial utopianism allows "pan-latinismo" to homogenize the Latino idea of ethnicity in the United States that hinders the battles against cultural and institutional prejudices against Hispanics of indigenous or African descent.[8] He provides as an example how U.S. Latino television networks such as Telemundo and Univisión use the idea of latinismo for profit, as they assimilate all Latino inhabitants into a group they can target for ads while continuing to promote a different take of white supremacy. This is evidenced in the fact that subaltern groups inside Latino communities (such as members of African and indigenous descent) are rarely featured in any of the shows the networks sell to sponsors.[9]

The differences between the contrasting perceptions of latinidad are addressed in the *Locas* saga itself, when Maggie and Hopey argue over their

Latino ethnic background in the seminal story "Wigwam Bam." This argument was so important to the plot development that it became one of the first steps in the decay of their utopian punk friendship. In the story, Maggie and Hopey are at a party (in an unspecified city on the East Coast) and they are annoyed by the pretensions of two artsy intellectuals. At some point one of the intellectuals asks Maggie if she is French but loses interest after learning she is Mexican.[10] Maggie becomes really irritated with the other guests later on when they are trying to remember her ethnicity and can barely distinguish between different representatives of what would be perceived as a dark brunette "other" in American society. Maggie complains to Hopey that the other party guests are racist, but Hopey only sees them as jerks and not as threatening prejudiced bigots. Maggie then screams at Hopey for her nonchalant attitude. Hopey, she claims, does not care about the insulting behavior of the intellectuals because, being only half-Mexican, she can pass as white. Her experience with whiteness is thus radically different to that of Maggie.[11]

Although scholar Todd Hignite partially attributes the collapse of Maggie and Hopey's relationship to the death of the nostalgic West Coast punk movement, in which both Gilbert and Jaime had participated, he also specifically explains how, by removing the characters from the comfort of their original California setting, Jaime was able to make them perceive the reality of race in a different manner:

> Location is a dominant character in Love and Rockets, and Hernandez chose a nameless East Coast city as the setting because he wanted them to be as far from Hoppers as possible, while still in the United States. The examination of ethnicity in different locales is an important underpinning, and characters are brought into sharper focus through conflicting reactions to their loss of cultural footing: "Some people allow their lives to change and others don't. It's obvious Maggie's a smalltown kid and all she wants to do is get home. Hopey is raised as a big city girl, and also was basically raised white, so the world is sort of her oyster. Maggie's not white, and so growing up, society is not her oyster—she's just allowed to live in it.[12]

It is important to discuss the nuances of how the different Latino subcultures are perceived if we try to define Los Bros' comics as Latino texts. Gilbert and Jaime Hernandez see themselves as Mexican Americans/Latinos and this is how they define themselves in interviews. However, when talking about other Latino artists who work in New York (as opposed to themselves, who do it in California and Nevada), they have referred to them as "Puerto Rican artists," thus establishing geographic and ethnic differences with them

Maggie and Hopey experience whiteness differently. Jaime Hernandez, *Perla la Loca*, 19. © Jamie Hernandez.

and their comic interests. For example, this is Gilbert's description of East Coast Latino comic book artists: "I see more of it in the mainstream comics. There are just more Latino writers, mostly artists, working in the field, simply because the big companies are in New York and they get Puerto Rican young people to work, and other ethnics as well."[13]

Clashing Latino aesthetics are featured in Los Bros' work, too. One of the most curious examples was related by Jaime during his open interview with Christopher González at Ohio State in 2013. According to Jaime, Dominican writer Junot Díaz was planning to republish his book *This Is How You Lose Her* after an editor suggested that Jaime provide illustrations for the new edition. They had collaborated before, when Jaime drew some visuals for a story by Junot Díaz that was published by the *New Yorker* ("The Pura Principle," March 22, 2010). After Jaime completed the illustrations for *This Is How You Lose Her*, the editor sent them to Díaz for approval and in a few days the latter returned them with a note to Jaime saying, "Draw them less Mexican." Jaime had tried to visualize the characters from the limited information provided in the prose, and of course the product looked like what he is accustomed to drawing from his own personal "Latino" experience.

This anecdote is interesting because Junot Díaz constantly quotes Los Bros as one of his main influences and *Love and Rockets* as the first Latino text in the United States with which he could identify, even though the stories were set mostly on the West Coast while he himself grew up on the East Coast.[14] This personal identification with Los Bros' work represents the latinismo/latinidad ideal that transcends specific Hispanic nationalisms. However, incompatibility issues certainly arose when Jaime's "Mexican-ness" affected the visual and racial representation of Junot's specifically Dominican characters, which in the end the author wanted the artist to fix.

The evolution of the hybrid Mexican American/Chicano/Latino narrative, which Gilbert and Jaime construct, is very difficult to map out if we use the idea of latinidad/latinismo. As Latino scholars tried to create a connection between different ethnic Latin American immigrants and their descendants while also invoking their different experiences with their respective original nation-states, their varied political situations in the United States have created some rifts in the Latino canon that are difficult to overcome. For example, the history and literature of Hispanic/Latino immigrants from the Caribbean in New York City or Miami, along with their geographical displacement and struggles with racism, have a different context to the Mexican American and Mexican immigrant bracero struggles in the Southwest. Modern American society and academia have had a tendency to package these struggles and experiences together in readers and classes under the umbrella of latinidad. However, the reality is that, in order to successfully discuss them together, one has to be aware of the similarities but also the differences that mark the various Hispanic ethnic groups' cultural production and transnationalism. As scholar Juan González writes, "Although all Latin Americans share the same general relationship to the United States, each nation's immigration story is unique in the times it occurred, the class and type of people who came, and the way they dealt with their new environment."[15]

The Chicano literary tradition that is part of the Latino movement may be key to understanding Los Bros' works, as it has shifted from employing a straightforward narrative strongly influenced by Marxist thought to a more postmodern approach in the last couple of decades. According to scholar Vernon E. Lattin, the main themes with which political Chicano literature originally engaged were as follows: "Thematically, the Chicano novel has been concerned with identity and ethnicity; the question of religious faith; the idea of Aztlan; a sense of the power of both the question of life and death and the cycle of existence; the conflicts of living as exploited people within a dominant Anglo society; migrant existence; the rural/urban dichotomy (the city as both destroyer and heaven); the importance of Mexico and the Mexican Revolution; a sense of cosmic hope; and a quest for mythic vision."[16]

Lattin also points out that initially some critics excluded from the Chicano canon early novels that covered some of these themes, such as *Pocho* and *Chicano*, for these works lacked cultural consciousness, did not identify with "la raza," and were too individualist, a critical assessment which many now consider unfair.[17] Lattin elaborates that Chicano identity had to be constructed by Latino authors in opposition to the United States hegemony as "this quest for self often involves a criticism of the socioeconomic injustices of the United States."[18] Following this ideological trend, scholars Héctor Calderón and José David Saldívar have described the original goal of Chicano studies in the following manner: "The tradition of Chicano literary studies that both of us inherited when we began our teaching and research careers in the early eighties was a product of the Chicano movement of the sixties, taking shape from a cultural and an institutional politics that called for the affirmation of a working class, Mexican-mestizo heritage as well as for the establishment of centers of research and curricular programs in the universities and colleges of the United States."[19] However, scholars such as Felipe D. Ortego y Gasca disagree with this conceptualization of Chicano studies, especially with its insistence on a specific Chicano experience, which I would say Calderón and Saldívar advocate by mentioning specific terms such as "mestizo heritage" and "working class." [20] It is also important to point out that not all of the Chicano movement literature has been written to be in dialectic opposition to Anglophone hegemony, and some examples such as Anaya's *Bless Me Ultima* and Ron Arias's *The Road to Tamazunchale* are more focused on other aspects of Latino culture.

Both Jaime and Gilbert have political content in their comics that I will explore in more detail in this chapter but that lack the dogmatism of some of the most radical Chicano literature from the 1960s that emphasized cultural and racial pride. When discussing their own political leanings, Los Bros acknowledge their superficial encounter with Marxism through some intellectual Chicano/Latino friends and recognize somewhat hazily the benefits of this ideology. For example, when asked by Gary Groth if he was interested in socialism, Gilbert responds, "I guess vaguely, superficially. I never read into it or anything. My friends were interested in it, and the basics things they talked about seemed logical to me—free public medical healthcare and stuff, those ideas made a lot of sense to me."[21]

Derek Parker Royal has written that for Los Bros, ethnicity is not the subject matter of their works, but rather a means of creating a narrative.[22] Gilbert has mentioned that his main goal was to create a narrative in which he could express the story of his childhood experiences and heritage that he found as interesting as anybody else's but without being boring and academic.[23] He specifically ridicules the interests of American intellectuals, who he says were only interested in Luis Buñuel's films as depositories of Mexican/Hispanic culture. As a consequence, this type of fine art film was the only Hispanic narrative shown in American theaters but, as Gilbert claims, "Nobody goes to those anyway."[24]

What I find attractive about Los Bros' approach is that they belong to a more contemporary generation of Mexican American/Latino artists who avoid certain problematic didactic tools that were previously often used to portray the Chicano/Latino experience in the times of segregation. Gilbert and Jaime understand the position of the Latino experience in relation to that of other ethnicities, which problematizes both the hegemony and the multicultural subalternity.[25] In addition, they construct appealing ethnic heroes that are flawed, and hegemonic characters that are simultaneously pathetic and sympathetic. This provides for a powerful dialogism, with which both Latino and Anglophone readers can interact, and that I already discussed in my analysis of Penny Century.

This balanced criticism of ethnic identity and politics is one of Los Bros' strengths.[26] In scholar Ana Merino's analysis of Gilbert's *Love and Rockets X*, she analyzes Igor, a half-Mexican, half-African American character, and finds that Gilbert wrote him as a more open-minded character than the characters of his ideologically conservative Mexican father and his borderline-racist Chicano friend Bobby. This is possibly a parody of the Chicano movement's romantic notions about *mestizaje*, which hides the racist trends that Torres-Saillant criticized. In Merino's words, "For Bobby, it is important that Igor chooses a racial space, whether he's Chicano or black. Though he engages Igor, he despises the blackness that makes part of Igor's bi-cultural roots. In return, Igor tries to have Bobby understand that such mind-set, bent on territorial power, only reproduces the hegemonic, repressive white model that prevails in the Third World. After he listens to Igor's argument, Bobby accuses him of being a *falso*, of acting like a whitey and not being *pura raza*."[27] This ambiguity about absolutes in race and class consciousness in Los Bros' work can be traced back to their punk/alternative comics influences. As briefly mentioned in the introduction of this book, many scholars have written about how Gilbert and Jaime's interactions with the punk scene influenced the creation, launch, and philosophy of *Love and Rockets*. In one of the interviews republished in *The Love and Rockets Companion*, they dedicate nine pages (21–29) to their taste in 1970s punk music and other relevant influential musicians. Gilbert mentions in the interview that he specifically enjoyed the subculture's ability to be "snotty and smart."[28] He also claims that punk music helped him develop his anarchic attitude that was essential in the launching of *Love and Rockets* as an independent book.[29]

Michelle Habell-Pallán, a scholar who in her book *Loca Motion* addressed the influence of punk in Chicano performance art, has provided some important critical statements that could help the reader better understand works such as *Love and Rockets*. She describes the similarities that existed between the traditional Chicano aesthetics that defied hegemony in the United States and the anarchist punk movement: "Like Chicana/o art, punk made space for critiques of social inequality and racism. Mainstream representations of punk represented punk culture as monolithic, yet punk had various and competing strains and was never only one thing. For Chicano artists, deploying punk sensibility and attitude was an early step in a larger engagement with the world at large."[30] Although she does not analyze specifically Los Bros' work within the context of the punk movement or of Chicano art in general, later in her book, Habell-Pallán relates how filmmaker Jim Mendiola praised *Love and Rockets* as an example in which "youth of color made the punk scene in their image and changed it themselves."[31]

Another contribution from the punk movement that is heavily emphasized by Habell-Pallán is how punk also helped to defy certain gender preconceptions. When discussing Marisela Norte's punk performance, she mentions how the artist's costume defied both Anglophone exoticism (by providing a cool and modern "noir look instead of Aztec flavor") and Chicano androcentric perceptions of womanhood (by dis-identifying with Chicano fantasies as elaborated in the first Chicano poem, "Yo soy Joaquín," and the poem's "black-shawled Faithful women"). Habell-Pallán notes further that if there was a Mexican influence in Norte's performance, it was the look of Maria Felix, the sharp-witted and sometimes cruel beauty of classic Mexican film.[32]

This particular statement is important to my analysis because it shows how Chicano/a artists influenced by punk used intertextual devices from both cultures to disrupt both traditional Chicano/Latino *and* hegemonic Anglophone discourse. For example, the relevance of the early "Mechan-X" sci-fi trappings in Jaime's *Locas* saga were important at the time in addressing the fact that Chicano/a Latino/a characters could be in the Anglophone genre comics as they also belong to modernity. However, Jaime defies the gender expectations of both Anglophone and Hispanic patriarchal traditions by depicting gay and lesbian sexuality, as well as by making Maggie a mechanic, a job usually associated with men in both cultures. In addition, the narrative featured a female point of view, a rarity in comics at the time (1980s).

Besides the Latina/Chicana punk movement, the breakaway from heteronormative boundaries is also relevant in Gloria Anzaldúa's *Frontera/Borderlands* and to her "new mestizo" theoretical concept that was developed by the author in 1987, a few years after the beginning of the publication of *Love and Rockets*. According to Sonia Saldívar-Hull, Anzaldúa still attached her writings to ideological/dialectic devices, as "autobiography for the new mestiza is the history of the colonization of indigenous Southwestern peoples by Anglo-American imperialists intent on their manifest destiny."[33] Saldívar-Hull goes on to explain that "Anzaldúa's project problematizes further still the traditions of Chicanismo, when, as a lesbian Chicana, she forces the homophobes of the Chicano community to see their prejudice."[34] The book has been important in the academic perception of feminism and ethnicity and the ambiguities of borderland culture, but these were already evident in Gilbert's *Palomar*, which reflects the changing perceptions of Chicano culture.

Next I will discuss how Gilbert's *Palomar* saga functions as an ironic and ambiguous Latino narrative, and how the immigration process is bizarrely represented in the story not as an intent to realistically portray transnational space but to address the evolution of the Latino narrative. I will discuss how Gilbert's ambiguous small-town *Palomar* narrative compares to Mexican comics that feature rural communities, such as Yolanda Vargas Dulché's *María Isabel* and Rius's *Los supermachos*. My intention is not to establish a link to Mexico as an epicenter of Mexican American culture and comics but to show how Gilbert's narrative embodies a mirror/parody of an imagined Latin American nation-state as a metaphor of the broadening and intertextual perceptions that Chicanos/Mexican American/Latinos have of themselves. I intend to show how a comic book writer/artist such as him is able to create a third space (as outlined by postcolonial thinkers) comic book that transcends the ideological binaries of both Mexican and United States narrative strategies.

The Latin American Imaginary and the Fictional Town of Palomar

When I first read Gilbert's *Palomar* stories, I felt very comfortable with his narrative because it resembled many "small-town" narratives I had previously encountered in Mexican or Latin American comics distributed in Puerto Rico in the 1980s. When discussing Los Bros' influences, American scholarship often mentions the direct influence of small-town narratives such as *Archie* and *Dennis the Menace*, which both brothers have acknowledged and that is visually obvious to readers. However, *Palomar*'s setting is outside of the United States, and therefore becomes a Mexican American/Latino representation of an imaginary foreign space that is also an imaginary point of origin for Gilbert as a Latino subject and an artist, and so it becomes important to explore how this representation fits within the small-town genre in Latin American comics too. That is why I will attempt to explain how Gilbert's town compares to those in more ideologically charged Mexican comic books such as Yolanda Vargas Dulché's *María Isabel* and Rius's *Los supermachos*. My goal is to analyze how the *Palomar* stories differ aesthetically and ideologically from these other comics that represent the two extremes of the Mexican state ideological spectrum.

In one of his interviews, Gilbert says that the ambiguity of *Palomar* has helped readers of other Latin American or Latino backgrounds connect with the story on a personal level because all of these readers can identify with his universal portrayal of Hispanic/Latino settings as they project themselves into the narrative.[35] This is partially due to the collective nostalgia of Latino readers in the United States for, even though they differ as a result of their specific national histories, Latin American small towns used to have similar physical and social infrastructures throughout the entire continent. Gilbert also creates a universal geographical fantasy due to the fact that Palomar borders a tropical forest, a desert, an ocean, and other types of physical spaces associated with Latin America.[36] However, I also found several aspects of this mythical small town different from real-world Latin American towns, such as Palomar's lack of benevolent/oppressive state authority figures and its representation as a utopian gynocentric society with an abundance of female leaders such as Luba and Chelo, the town mayor and sheriff, respectively.

When asked by Gary Groth if he researched Central America to narrate the story set in Palomar, Gilbert replied, "No, no, if there's one thing I can't stand, it's research. That's another reason why Palomar is an imaginary town, because I'd hate to do the research."[37] This particular statement is very important because it shows that as a Latino artist, Gilbert is not interested in the realist approach of some other Chicano narratives that re-create accurately transnational space and affect politically the representation of other nation-states.

Gilbert has admitted that he has received some criticism about his *Palomar* stories because of the lack of controversial Latin American social institutions (for example, the Catholic Church or dictatorships) that are constantly criticized by leftist thinkers. His response, as recorded in an interview with Frederick Aldama, was the following:

> I've been asked before, how come the Catholic Church isn't more involved in your story? How come the government's not involved? How come the men aren't as macho as they should be? Well, I say, if you already know that, why are you asking me? If you know that the Catholic Church is already this, that Latino men are like this, why do you need to see it on paper? Why do you need to know what you already know? My goal is to show the reader that Latinos are people. That's my job.[38]

This debate about the Catholic Church is interesting because it shows the transnational divide about the perceptions of Latino culture. When Gary Groth asked the two brothers about their experience with the Catholic Church, they responded that they tried to go but in the end they could not take it seriously once their sexuality was awakened. This statement clarifies that Los Bros' rift with the church was not the consequence of their joining a political cause but was the result of individual biological necessities.[39] For many Latin American readers, however, the Catholic Church is an important element in the history of their countries and it may be perceived negatively or positively depending on the role of Catholicism in the development of a particular Latin American nation-state. Gilbert does not understand why, if it is already clear to readers that the Catholic Church is "evil," they still need to see his art reflect this perception. Yet readers likely expect literary narratives to reflect and support a certain ideology about their state and their ruling hegemony, and to them the narrative falls short of providing evidence for that.

Gilbert might not subscribe to an ideology within the nation-state apparatus, yet I argue that there is indeed political conflict in his *Palomar* stories. However, originally this conflict was situated for the most part outside of the writer's "idealized" town, and it is only hinted at until being fully developed in the prequel, *Poison River*. Because Palomar is not situated in a specific nation-state, most of the political and cultural history of the town is completely absent, so there are no references to a national history, real institutions, or real-life historical figures, all generally important elements in constructing an ideological historical narrative of a nation-state. The conflicts emphasized here are centered predominantly around the antagonism created by frustrated sexual desires and gender issues rather than over ethnic/class conflict. Even in *Poison River*, where Gilbert addresses the political conflict, the main object of the characters is ultimately the fulfillment of desire.

In her excellent article "Picturing the Transnational in Palomar," scholar Jennifer Glaser explains that "the work of the Hernandez brothers (as comics artists Gilbert, Jaime, and Mario Hernandez have come to be called) has long provided an important space for the analysis of the making of transnational identities."[40] To me, the key word here is identity, as *Palomar* cannot embody the real history of a specific nation-state and its specific ideologies but rather reflect the nostalgic notion of the author's identity and his quest to represent that emigration pattern that led to his own transnational self. This nostalgia for an imaginary space where they are the mainstream is what all Latinos in the United States may identify with while reading the *Palomar* saga.

The portrayal of the imaginary past was addressed by Frederick Aldama when he directly asked Gilbert Hernandez about the reasons for setting *Palomar* in the imaginary "south of the border." Gilbert's response is to link the idea to his Mexican father and heritage but not to the state:

> My family's tree starts in Mexico, so why not start this story from the egg.
> Dad's from Mexico, Mom's from that part of Texas that used to be Mexico,
> and I'm born here, so I'll start with a little village, and then one day have
> the characters cross the border. Then I'll tell stories about their experience
> on the U.S. side of the border. While I projected that far ahead in the story,
> I knew that I would have to create a solid foundation so all of these future
> stories, like those that make up Luba in America, would stand strong.[41]

In an interview with Darcy Sullivan, Gilbert further acknowledges the lack of realism in the visual construction of the town. He says that he copied some town visuals from watching Spanish-speaking channels on TV, specifically movies from the 1950s and '70s, as reference books were hard to come by.[42] He adds that "In a way, Palomar is more of a version of Southern California than of Latin America, because all the different styles of buildings are smashed together. I never make it clear if it's a new town or an old town. It's a total fantasy place."[43] This is a very important quote, where he specifically acknowledges that he is not representing another nation-state but rather a borderland narrative that does not fit in between the Mexican and American national spaces. This conceptual ambiguity can be debatable, and Jennifer Glaser has wondered "how might the space of Latino comics function as an analogue for the space of the nation or, more precisely, the 'borderlands' that Anzaldúa sees as a productive aesthetic and ontological space between nations?"[44]

In an interview originally published by *The Comics Journal* and reprinted in *The Love and Rockets Companion*, Gilbert explains the narrative transition from the bizarre sci-fi parody "BEM" that was published in the first issue of *Love and Rockets* (and discussed in chapter 1) into the more grounded *Palomar* saga. He mentions that Palomar's first story, "Heartbreak Soup," was supposed to be a sequel to "BEM," at the end of which Luba has become a revolutionary. Luba was to be hiding in Palomar after the rebels removed her from their leadership, and the BEM character was to reappear at the end of the story. However, Gilbert changed his mind and took the opportunity to do something "realistic," which he knew his editor Gary Groth would support even if some fans would be disappointed by the genre shift.[45]

What is interesting about this statement is that Gilbert's realism involves refusing to enter into the politics or ideology (as he removed the rebel plot) of the imaginary nation-state. From an American comic book perspective, realism meant less science fiction (like in "BEM") and simply portraying ordinary people with ordinary problems that are not related to political institutions. This is a valid approach, as by depoliticizing the story and emphasizing the neurotic elements of sexuality, it could become easier for the non-Latino reader to identify with the plots and characters. However, many cultural critics would have issues and possibly dismiss this approach as an anarchist point of view that lacks a clear ideological message that was relevant in the social struggles of the 1960s.

On the other hand, it is sometimes difficult to assess the goals of Latino representations outside/inside of the United States. Scholar Bill Ashcroft mentions that Latino diasporas are marked by transnationalism because they must exist and construct themselves outside of the parameters of their original nation-state.[46] However, these experiences can be marked differently by how the Latino author perceives himself/herself, which is why scholar Nicolás Kanellos in his article "Exiles, Immigrants, and Natives" tries to define three categories into which to group Latino narratives developed while presenting the history of Hispanic publishing in the United States. These three subgroups are the exiled, the immigrant, and the native. According to Kanellos, exiled authors were among the first to write in the United States and did not see themselves as part of the United States but were instead more worried in creating political change in their country of origin to which they hoped to return one day. Their initial texts were more about "providing information and opinion about the homeland, changing or solidifying opinion about politics in the *patria,* assisting in raising funds to overthrow the current regime, and providing ideological base for the overthrow."[47]

Kanellos also explores in his article the differences brought about by immigrant readers, many of whom did not necessarily want to return to their homeland but tried to re-create their culture and community in their new state while resisting assimilation, a process that sometimes led to isolation from the mainstream.[48] In contrast, the native Latino author knew his reality was to live in the United States but tried to see how he could affect the United States into accepting his cultural heritage while fully embracing his reality and identity as part of a U.S. minority group and while interacting with the Anglophone culture as well.[49] One of the main goals of this chapter is to show how both Gilbert and Jaime belong to this last subgroup, the native Latino, as their sagas seek to integrate important aspects of Latino culture into Anglophone comic traditions in order to create change without being assimilated into the discourse of either American or Mexican hegemonies.

One of the ways in which Palomar's ambiguity could be good for the story is through its avoidance of long-distance nationalism as conceptualized by Benedict Anderson.[50] This long-distance nationalism has been part of some segments of pan-Latino culture, and the concept applies well to some of the literature written in the United States. Some books by immigrants or native Latinos who have tried to reconstruct the history and culture of their Latin American state of origin (such as Julia Alvarez's depiction of the Trujillo dictatorship in the Dominican Republic) are better received than others, but they always remain controversial due to the ideological subjectivity of the author, the targeted readership, or the debates about cultural and historical accuracy.[51]

As I mentioned in the first chapter, Gilbert's first story in *Love and Rockets* ("BEM") also had an ambiguous setting in the fictional San Sassafras. Here, Gilbert introduced two characters from his future *Palomar* saga (Peter and Luba), but the plot does not fit with the later continuity, which is why "BEM" is not included in the *Palomar* canon. The more down-to-earth town of Palomar and its cast of characters were introduced in *Love and Rockets: New Stories # 3* with "Heartbreak Soup," or "Sopa de la gran pena," as Gilbert translates himself on the second page. Interestingly, Gilbert's "Heartbreak Soup" does not make much sense in English but it does sounds like wordplay on the Hispanic mispronunciation of "heartbreak soap." As a consequence, the translation in Spanish, "Sopa de la gran pena," does not make sense either, as if Gilbert is warning us that this is his U.S. Latino vision of Latin

America that is not intended to be accurate. It is almost as if he is self-aware of how his depiction lacks the "authenticity" some readers may assume the text has, just because he is of a Latino or Mexican descent.

Still, because Gilbert himself linked his *Palomar* narrative to the soap genre from the beginning with the title "Heartbreak Soup," this narrative is often perceived as a soap opera by critics and fans. While introducing his robot adventure *Citizen Rex*, Gilbert's older brother Mario mentioned that a fan at a convention was not impressed by his work and told his friends that "*Love and Rockets* is nothing but a soap opera," to which Mario responded "but hey, it is a well drawn soap!"[52]

When fans and critics toss the word "soap" around, it often seems they assume that Gilbert and Jaime's works belong to this genre because of their Latino heritage. In fact, radio soaps began in the United States, and this narrative concept has evolved differently in Latin America. In her book *Melodrama*, Brazilian scholar Silvia Oroz traces contemporary Western melodramatic plot devices to eighteenth-century bourgeois French theater and European literature. During the nineteenth century, the masses gained access to these narratives through the newspaper serials that became widely popular and, despite the change in readership, continued to uphold bourgeois values and to feature plots revolving around the idea of family in modern society. In the twentieth century, the American soap industry began to sponsor radio versions of these narratives that gained even larger audiences because the listeners did not need to know how to read and because it was easier to disseminate stories through airwaves than paper. These radio shows have influenced serial literature in general, including comics, television shows, and other types of modern narratives.[53]

In their book *The Soap Opera*, Muriel Cantor and Suzanne Pingree define soap operas as serial narratives about ordinary people and their domestic problems, which is why the genre tends to be universal.[54] As often happens to readers of Los Bros' comics, the soap opera viewer may not have experienced the beginning of the plot and may have to unravel the stories without the help of the author.[55] Cantor and Pingree also mention that some of the soaps never end and that the completion of their narrative may lead to another one.[56] The researchers establish further that one of the main differences between the American and Latin American soaps (telenovelas) is their length. Latin American telenovelas have a shorter production span and only last a few years at most, while American soaps can continue for decades.[57] One could say that both Gilbert and Jaime follow the American model because neither the *Palomar* nor the *Locas* sagas has a definite end, and Los Bros have been quoted as saying that they will continue to publish these series until there are no customers left (see my interview with them).

While Los Bros' narratives structurally fit better into the American soap opera model, the subject of life in a small town (Palomar) in a Latin American nation-state would have been encountered by a U.S. Latino audience through the telenovela model or through Latin American melodramas distributed on Spanish-language broadcast networks in the United States. These latter narratives undoubtedly influenced Los Bros' work, even on the most basic visual level—for example, what Palomar looks like (as quoted earlier). The brothers might not have the personal experience of living and working in Mexico, yet they use some of the settings, tropes, and devices that are widespread in Mexican soap opera/telenovela narratives. I will now outline the intersections of Gilbert's *Palomar* stories with the most iconic Mexican comic book small-town narratives in order to demonstrate how Los Bros function within the United States without subscribing to national ideology and also share part of the cultural tradition of Mexico, yet again without subscribing to the two extremes of Mexican revolutionary ideology.

Yolanda Vargas Dulché's *María Isabel* is the best example of a Mexican comic book narrative in the style of a soap opera/telenovela that I can use to compare with Gilbert's *Palomar* saga. This storyline was published in Vargas Dulché's popular comic *Lágrimas y Risas* in 1964 and had only forty-nine episodes. *Lágrimas* sales were among the highest in the Mexican comic book industry, and many of Vargas Dulché's stories published in this anthology series (such as *Rubí* and *Gabriel y Gabriela*) were later adapted into films and telenovelas. *María Isabel* itself was among the most popular ones, and it was adapted into a two-part feature film (*María Isabel*, 1968, and *El amor de María Isabel*, 1970) starring famous actress Sylvia Pinal, as well as into two different telenovelas in 1966 and 1997.

I think *María Isabel* can be compared to the *Palomar* saga because it also begins in a small town and shows the evolution of a female protagonist (María Isabel) of an indigenous (and mestizo) heritage from a poor peasant to a sophisticated member of the bourgeoisie. Toward the end of the story she is able to achieve economic success and happiness by moving to France. This narrative structure is very similar to the experience of Gilbert's Luba and her family, who, after suffering many problems and heartbreaks, finally achieve a more elite status once they move to the United States and become financially successful with their businesses.

Despite the similar melodramatic plotlines, however, the difference between the two texts is both formalistic and ideological. First, *María Isabel* is a shorter storyline (49 chapters), like a telenovela, while Gilbert's *Palomar* saga's length is more similar to American soaps such as *General Hospital*. In addition, María Isabel's social mobility is visualized through a more conservative/traditional lens, where chastity and belief in the system (the Catholic Church and Mexican intellectual bourgeoisie) are rewarded, while Luba and her family's lives are explored through Gilbert's more anarchic point of view, in which rampant sexuality is what releases the characters from oppression.

In their book *Not Just for Children: The Mexican Comic Book in the Late 1960s and 1970s*, scholars Harold E. Hinds Jr. and Charles Tatum dedicate a chapter to *Lágrimas y Risas* and explain how this comic was the second most popular comic in Latin America after the Orientalist Mexican hero *Kalimán*. Because of the lack of statistical data on the Mexican comic book industry, they interviewed several sellers in Mexico about who the main customers for this type of storytelling were, and many answered that it was women of working- and middle-class background. In Mexico, as in other countries (for example, Japan's *shoujo* genre), a substantial portion of the comic book market targeted specifically female audiences, something that is not the case with the U.S. market.

Hinds and Tatum explore in their book the conservative values embedded in *Lágrimas y Risas*. Many of the plots in the anthology are repetitive, as expected from the modern culture industry, and the characters are visualized with a white/European aesthetic that was used in Mexico at the time. The mestizos included in Vargas Dulché's narrative are limited to working-class secondary roles as maids, servants, criminals, and so forth:

> Virtually without exception the main characters, whether young or old, male or female, have no traces of Mexican Indian physical traits and in only a few instances could characters identify as mestizo (persons of mixed European and Indian ancestry). Although the creators of the comic politely but firmly declined to comment on their characters' physical traits or on their motives for creating a largely non-mestizo world, clearly they did not intend to reproduce the ethnic and racial character of contemporary Mexico. If this realism had been their intent, the creators of Lágrimas would have populated the pages of the comic book with a more representative mix of European, mestizo, Mexican Indian characters.[58]

Scholars Cantor and Pingree observe that soap operas that target housewives or working-class women tend to be conservative because that type of audience prefers more idealized notions about their lives that focus on problems that could be solved on a personal level rather than the feminist or revolutionary didacticism that can be found in more progressive/class-conscious/oppositional narratives.[59] Hinds and Tatum write that specifically in *Lágrimas* one could not find any reference to the tumultuous Mexico of the 1960s and '70s or to homosexuality, women's movements, or the student movement.[60] When compared to Gilbert's *Palomar*, at first glance *Lágrimas* seems more grounded in Mexican reality because it is set in Mexico, features Mexican characters, and identifiable Mexican visuals. Paradoxically, however, Gilbert's *Palomar* is the narrative that includes references to the ideological struggles relevant to recent Mexican history, even though it is supposedly set in an imaginary country.

Among the different *Lágrimas y Risas* narratives, *María Isabel* is the one that stands out with its mestiza heroine and the inclusion of some indigenous characters for at least the beginning of the storyline. The plot is set in a small town similar to Gilbert's Palomar and features a rigid class structure that is represented by the power of the rich plantation owner Don Félix. In the story, María Isabel is described as the most beautiful woman of indigenous ancestry in the town (probably because she is drawn with European features).[61] She befriends Don Félix's daughter Graciela and their friendship would overcome social, racial, and class boundaries but in the process destroy both characters' lives and their relationship with their respective parents. Graciela dies of grief when her boyfriend is killed by her father, but not before she entrusts her blond daughter to María Isabel. This trust from a Caucasian mother who prefers the indigenous but pure María Isabel over her evil landowner father embodies one of the utopian ideals often promoted by the Mexican Revolution.[62]

Even though the comic could be perceived as crude melodrama, there are elements of Bakhtin's dialogism in play as characters' perspectives collide, and both the masculine indigenous and the hegemonic discourses are defied by María Isabel and Graciela from a feminine point of view. María Isabel is a heroine of the people, who first clashes with the feudalistic landowner and then with the conniving bourgeoisie that live in the Mexican capital and in France. Of course, as this is a commercial mass culture series, the writing leads to an incredible happy ending that would disturb many progressive intellectuals because its main goal is to assimilate the character of María Isabel into the bourgeoisie and erase her "Indian-ness."[63] Visual aesthetic choices are important in achieving this, as the heroine is perceived as beautiful in the story because she is drawn as a white woman. Her indigenous features are ethnic and not racial, which becomes more evident when her "European" looks are juxtaposed to the facial and body features of the other indigenous characters. This racist visualization has been translated to the María Isabel film and soap opera adaptations, where the character is played by white (and sometimes even blond) Mexican actresses.

The representation of María Isabel reflects the postrevolutionary Mexican government's attempts to integrate the Indian/mestizo into the fabric of Mexican society. Gilbert's Luba is a different depiction of the mestizo/a ideal that is part of Latino nostalgia about the culture inherited from Latin American nation-states. Gilbert emphasizes her indigenous features as part of her beauty and sex appeal. Unlike the *María Isabel* comics, the protagonist in *Palomar* is not ashamed of being mestiza. This is a general trend in Chicano narratives, as observed by Rafael Perez Torres in his book *Mestizaje*, where he writes, "If, then, mestizaje in Mexico represents a flight from the Indian, we might think of Chicana mestizaje as a race toward the Indian."[64]

Gilbert's depiction, however, is not sentimental or nostalgic, as he presents several scenes in which the Palomar residents are racist to the characters immersed in indigenous culture, as visualized through the latter's clothing and behavior. According to Jennifer Glaser, Gilbert's ideal of hybridity is conflicting, for it makes Luba both powerful and pathetic:

> Race and the representation of race remain fundamental facts of life in Palomar. Luba, the de facto leader of Palomar, inhabits such a powerful, yet vexed, role in the town in part because of her half-Indian racial heritage. Born of an upwardly mobile, light-skinned woman who soon escapes to the US and an Indian worker, Luba represents the mestiza consciousness of Central America. Known as "La India," her darker complexion, wild hair (which her cousin Ofelia mocks in "An American in Palomar"), and protuberant breasts make her both an object of lust for Palomar's residents and an object of ridicule when she ventures outside of town to the larger city area. Luba's power comes in part from her invocation of the spectral Indian that haunts postcolonial Central America.[65]

One could say that besides the differences between the mestiza heroines, Gilbert's *Palomar* saga shares certain elements with the "wholesome" *María Isabel*. As a sentimental story, *María Isabel* is the perfect soap/telenovela comic in which Yolanda Vargas Dulché tried to make hegemonic Mexican society identify with the plight of the poor indigenous communities. Gilbert's goal is similar: to make Anglophone readers identify with the imaginary citizens of a small Latin American town that serve as a metaphor for the ostracized Chicano/Mexican American communities in the United States. Vargas Dulché achieved this emotional attachment with a concise and accessible serialized story, which she merged with the beautiful and visually stunning aesthetic of Antonio Gutiérrez's drawings. Gutiérrez's art works for a mass audience because it mimics the cinema and television melodramas and soap operas to which readers/viewers are accustomed, with the constant use of close-ups to depict the feelings of the characters and therefore engage the audience emotionally.

This cinematic approach is also present in Gilbert's saga, as Charles Hatfield observes:

> His work recalls traditional narrative cinema in specific ways, mimicking the movie camera's capacity for naturalism, intimacy, and movement. The artist himself, while distinguishing between film and comics, acknowledges his reliance on movies as "the best visual reference as far as capturing a scene" (Hernandez to author), an admission that sheds light on his habits of panel composition. In fact Hernandez's panels favor certain filmic devices, which he uses to pose characters in close relation both to the reader and to each other: extreme close-ups, close two-shots, foreground framing, and deep focus, that is, extreme depth of field.[66]

However, the main difference between Gutiérrez's and Gilbert's melodramatic visuals is that Gutiérrez's attempt at mimicking live action photography and the frequent close-ups used in telenovelas make his drawings beautiful but stiff due to the absence of movement in the panel-to-panel transitions. In contrast, as Charles Hatfield has mentioned, Gilbert reconciles the realistic devices with the various means of caricature abstraction, which allows him to manipulate the images in order to achieve humor and irony more effectively inside his melodramatic structure.[67]

Even though Vargas Dulché's comics are aesthetically excellent, Mexican academics prefer the works of other Mexican cartoonists, like the legendary comic book artist Rius, who attempted to deconstruct Mexican nationalist propaganda and create a more class-conscious vision of the country. One of the most famous Mexican comics about life in small-town Mexico is Rius's *Los supermachos*, originally published in the 1960s and set in San Garabato, a fictional Mexican small town very similar to Gilbert's Palomar.[68] The story features a multicharacter cast, and characters of indigenous heritage are portrayed as the victims of the oppressive political system, which includes the mayor (who constantly follows orders coming from the federal government), the Spanish immigrant and owner of the local grocery store, the police officer, and the fanatical Catholic women who spy on the rest of the town in order to help the church uphold conservative values. The only middle-class character who is portrayed with a little empathy is Don Lucas, an intellectual who runs the local pharmacy. However, he can be a bumbling fool who is ineffective in opposing the hegemonic system set up by the Mexican federal government.

Rius's comic art is not as aesthetically pleasing as Antonio Gutierrez's or Gilbert's art, but his contributions to the political cartoon are very innovative due to his gritty unpolished visual re-creation of the small town and its social problems. His topics were based on controversial subjects linked to real political and historical events that were taking place in Mexico, and the final product was very different to other popular comics such as Yolanda Vargas Dulché's *María Isabel*. Throughout most of *Los supermachos*, Rius's critique attempted to subvert the values of the Mexican Revolution and the hegemony of a state that subscribes to hypocritical social values, namely, the pretense that they are helping the indigenous population. For example, in one of his stories in *Supermachos* 27 (reprinted in *Mis supermachos*, vol. 3), the government is sponsoring art exhibitions in the small towns to educate the masses. What sounds like a well-intentioned, albeit paternalistic, goal from the federal government is satirized through the incompetence of the mayor of the town (the government's representative), who is as ignorant about the arts as the indigenous population that the revolutionary government is supposed to be helping. In the end, many of the poor townsfolk would have preferred more help with food, alcohol, or work, than the fine arts pretensions imposed by the people in the capital.

Even though I love Rius's attacks on "the system," I have to admit that his comics can be condescending from the point of view of an intellectual. Scholar David Foster in his book *From Mafalda to the Supermachos* confirms this perception when he writes about how Rius mocks institutions and values while displaying a snob attitude toward the masses:

> The "author" (in reality, an unidentified team of Meridiano employees) assumes the right to satirize mercilessly values and beliefs that are, to one degree or another, popular, with the clear implication that anyone who subscribes to them must be stupid. Complicity in this belief is invited from the reader of any one of Mexico's social strata. The allies of the author thus have by implication both the right and the duty to mock and repudiate such values by virtue of their presupposed analytical superiority, which legitimatizes the ironic scrutiny of the "simple folk." In this sense, the satirizing of national values cannot help but be also the putting down of aspects of the popular masses.[69]

One of the main differences between Rius's San Garabato and Gilbert's Palomar is the depiction of authority figures. In *Los supermachos*, there is a clear depiction of Mexican authorities that range from government officials, to religious fanatics of the Catholic Church, to the Mexican bourgeoisie. Through the character of Mexican Indian Calzonzín, Rius establishes opposition to the hegemony's views through the point of view of the oppressed. This clash between the oppressor and the oppressed is featured in every story and always concludes with a lesson to the reader about the flaws of the Mexican government under capitalism. In contrast, institutions that Rius constantly attacks, such as the Catholic Church, the government, and the rich in power, are rarely featured in Gilbert's Palomar. In Gilbert's town, the sheriff position is most of the time occupied by Chelo, a tough female character who sometimes imposes her puritanical values about clothing but has a lot of sex in the privacy of her home and is open-minded enough not to out Luba's daughter Maricela when she sees her kissing another girl on the beach.[70] Luba herself is a female mayor who owns the local bathhouse and theater but does not oppress the people in town or look to exploit them economically.

Rius's stories about San Garabato and Gilbert's, about Palomar, differ in themes, politics, and aesthetics. First, because Gilbert does not disclose the official location of Palomar, his appraisal of its fictional nation-state is not historicized, nor does it directly represent real events linked to a particular country, in contrast to Rius's very Mexican storylines. Second, Gilbert's story does not follow the repetitive elements of comedic cartoons in which characters never change and each issue follows a similar structure. Visually, Gilbert's art is more refined than the grungy and distorted art by Rius, and his approach resembles more an epic soap than just a series of skits relying on slapstick humor. Third, as previously stated, Gilbert is more interested in exploring the neurotic aspects of his small-town society and how they are linked to sexual repression and desires rather than their conflict with a hegemonic institution. In an ironic way, the use of sex in Gilbert's *Palomar* stories is what situates his narrative in a subversive third sexual space outside of the Mexican binaries represented by *María Isabel* and *Los supermachos*.

Even though Gilbert's early stories do not contain obvious historical references, American critics often find politics in his *Palomar* saga. For example, Jennifer Glaser writes that "the mythology he creates in the village of Palomar is not the ahistorical sort of conventional myth. Instead, Hernandez's terra incognita proves distinctly historical and politicized. Even if Palomar is constructed to be a world in which all (Latino) readers can see themselves, it is nonetheless a world inscribed with the palimpsest of Latin and Central

American history—its unique history of colonial domination and racial hierarchy and mixture."[71] Charles Hatfield also observes that the *Palomar* saga evolves into a more political text with the *Poison River* storyline, which "differs from prior *Heartbreak Soup* stories in that it engages more directly with the sociopolitical realities and myths of modern-day Latin America. It seems more embedded in the traumas of history than the tales that take place in Palomar's frankly synthetic locale."[72]

Before *Poison River,* capitalism affects the locals in Gilbert's *Palomar* only in a few random cases, such as when the character of Gato fires some of his friends from the local factory because he is a corporate stooge. However, Gato's flaws can be interpreted as related to his weak character rather than as a denunciation of the evils of capitalism. For example, Gato's ex-wife Pipo, one of the brightest characters in *Palomar*, is portrayed as an excellent capitalist who succeeds in the United States and supports the town of Palomar economically even though she no longer lives there. What is interesting about these female authority figures is that they are powerful women who are very comfortable with their sexuality, which is why they are very assertive. Their beliefs and actions could actually be perceived as controversial (for example, Luba is not too happy about some of her daughters' lesbian sexual orientation, and Pipo lives a decadent lifestyle in the United States), but it is easy to admire their independence from relying on any government or patriarchal institution.

Both Yolanda Vargas Dulché's *María Isabel* and Rius's *Los supermachos* predate the sexual revolution, so the exploration of sexuality is not one of their main concerns. Alternative artists such as Gilbert and Jaime were directly influenced by the comix movement developed during the sexual revolution, and their work is more explicitly related to the changes in society's perceptions of sexuality and its manifestation. Leftist artists such as Rius would not always be comfortable using sexuality to disrupt hegemonic morality and institutions. When Hinds and Tatum discuss Rius's contributions to the political cartoon in Mexico, they find a counterpart to it in the American underground comix movement that I discussed in chapter 1. Rius himself was familiar with comix and found them interesting, but did not approve of their absence of political focus and their frequent degeneration into pornography.[73] Los Bros' *Love and Rockets* sometimes is similarly criticized for its uncommitted politics and erotic qualities that may be a remnant of the influence of the American underground movement that developed in California.

Gilbert's *Palomar* shares some connections with iconic Mexican comic book texts, such as *María Isabel* and *Los supermachos*, even though the author himself acknowledges that he has not read Mexican comics because he does not speak Spanish. Nevertheless, he is aware of their existence on a purely visual level through the comics his brother Mario read and films he himself has seen. The imaginary he is trying to visualize thus has some similarities with what the Mexicans had been producing but, because Gilbert was raised on the West Coast, he has a different approach to the small-town topic, particularly in his depiction of female authority figures and their sexuality.

Sexual Frustration and the Intellectual in Palomar

One of the most distinctive aspects of Gilbert's *Palomar* universe is the intellectual portrayed in it as a tragic catalyst of change. Gilbert recognizes the intellectuals' importance and how they have the ability to open the "eyes of the people," but at the same time he portrays their inability to handle sexuality as one of the causes of their downfall. The first intellectual character who destroys himself in Gilbert's narrative is Soledad. He is portrayed as having read some books and being smart but overweight (and thus not very physically attractive). He also practically commits an act of pedophilia by buying a dress for the underage Pipo and convincing her to have sex with him. He remains unhappy even after this intimate encounter, a behavior that the townsfolk attribute to his disappointment with Pipo. The girl had sex with him for money, yet also slept with his friend Manuel but without any material incentive.

Soledad's dissatisfaction with his own life is further revealed when he returns from a brief stint in the United States. Everyone is curious to know if he went to Disney World, one of the few places in the United States of which Palomar residents have heard. Soledad's answer is never provided directly, but townsfolk relate that he did go to Disney World and hated it as much as he hated the United States itself. The other characters care little about his attitudes, and the character of Israel assumes he is just angry because he probably "was too fat to fit in the rides."[74]

Ironically, Soledad's grievance is later revealed to be the consequence of his sexual obsession with his friend Manuel and not his disappointment with Pipo or the United States. At the end of the story, he shoots and kills Manuel in a queer crime of passion that also involves the underage Pipo in the love triangle. As Manuel is dying, he thinks Soledad killed him over the female subject (as would happen in traditional narratives), but Soledad reveals the violence is brought about by his fixation with the homosexual relationship they had had in the past. All the knowledge in the world did not solve Soledad's issues with sexuality, and after he is arrested, we never hear about him again in the *Palomar* saga.[75]

Palomar residents dismiss Soledad's intellectualism. Gilbert Hernandez, *Heartbreak Soup*, 39. © Gilbert Hernandez.

Another important intellectual character is Luba's cousin Ofelia. When she is introduced, she already has reached an advanced age and is portrayed as a less powerful figure who helps Luba run her businesses and raise her many children. Her intellectualism is hinted at through the fact that she reads complex books to the children, such as Victor Hugo's *Les Misérables*, and scares them with stories about how the Inquisition crushed Galileo's dreams.[76] She constantly complains about Luba's sexual escapades while remaining an "old maid" herself.

Ofelia loses her power over Luba in *Poison River* when she is raped and brutally beaten, while her best friends are also raped and then murdered. After barely surviving the attack herself, she disappears from the story, but comes back toward the end in a less dominant position to Luba. What is interesting about Ofelia is that she is able to gain some confidence when she rediscovers her sexuality. When she returns towards the end of *Poison River*, she has a bad back due to the brutal attack she suffered at the hands of the right-wingers. However, when she joins a hippie commune with Luba, they engage in constant sex with the members of the commune and her back spasms disappear. As Ofelia grows older and no longer has a sexual partner, she regresses into complaining and harassing Luba's daughters with her intellectualism. Later, when the whole family moves into the United States, the traditional old-fashioned literary person that she is threatens to write a book

Carmen struggles to read *One Hundred Years of Solitude*. Gilbert Hernandez, *Heartbreak Soup*, 222. © Gilbert Hernandez.

about Luba to disclose all of her secrets. This plot is one of the main events in Luba's family life, until Ofelia finds one of her former boyfriends and decides to elope with him, thus abandoning her vindictive project.

The last important intellectual character in *Palomar* is Heraclio. As narrated in the story "For the Love of Carmen," Heraclio was raised in Palomar but he studied at a university, where he earned a music degree.[77] He bonded with his university friends, as intellectuals often do, but never felt part of their clique because they were from the big cities and made fun of his small-town origins. When he was fifteen, he was sexually molested by Luba, and

Revision of Latino Experience through Comic Book Genres and Soap Opera Devices he fathered her daughter Guadalupe. This "rape" is his shameful secret and marked his life as a nonassertive man who later married Carmen, one of the most feisty locals. His relationship with his wife is somewhat strained because, even though he loves her, she does not share his intellectual habits.

One of the most interesting scenes about their relationship reveals how Heraclio's intellectualism has driven a wedge in their marriage, and his wife tries to read his favorite book, Gabriel García Márquez's *One Hundred Years of Solitude*, in order to get closer to him. She struggles with a single sentence that she reads at random, only to become quickly discouraged by the author's literary devices.[78]

Carmen's isolation and her inability to communicate with her husband are powerfully portrayed in this sequence of textless (with the exception of the sentence she bungles) panels in which the visibly distraught woman tries to get physically close to the books. She moves across the room to the bookshelf, her hand shown in close-up picking up a tome. Unable to read it, she puts it back, leaning against the black shadow of a shelf looming over her. Carmen fails to understand her estranged husband through the author he likes, despite her efforts. Ironically, however, the book does not bring Heraclio close to the female intellectual friend that she is afraid would "steal" him either. Just like Carmen, Gloria does not like García Márquez's book, but for precisely the opposite reason. She thinks *One Hundred Years of Solitude* is inferior, repetitive, and childish fiction when compared to the works of great writers such as Dostoyevsky.[79]

Heraclio's role in Gilbert's acclaimed "Human Diastrophism" storyline is very important because he is the mentor of Humberto, a talented young painter. This young man develops his artistic techniques under Heraclio's guidance but fails to develop a political consciousness. He knows who the serial killer murdering Palomar residents is, but does not act or disclose the information to the authorities. He is just fascinated by the gruesome acts and indulges in the aestheticization of the events by painting the murders. In the end, when it is discovered that he knew the identity of the serial killer, he is banished from creating art ever again. According to Charles Hatfield, Humberto represents a very important statement about modernist art, as, through Humberto, Hernandez questions the power of art to intervene in social and political crises and probes the issue of the artist's social liability.[80] On the other hand, Gilbert juxtaposes this disconnect with the bizarre and extreme political commitment of a character such as Tonatzin, who becomes so involved with all the political events that are happening in the world that she lights herself on fire to protest the evils of capitalist and imperial hegemony.

Gloria dismisses *One Hundred Years of Solitude* as subpar literature. Gilbert Hernandez, *Heartbreak Soup*, 216. © Gilbert Hernandez.

Both bourgeois detachment and extreme political commitment are destructive in different ways.

When I asked Gilbert why he parodied the powerlessness of his Latino intellectual characters in the *Palomar* saga, he rejected the notion, as he is fond of the characters, and it seems he assumed that parody meant hatred or negative assessment. The reason I felt his depiction of the intellectual was important in my analysis of his stories is that to me, Soledad, Ofelia, and Heraclio represent how the subversive Latino thought had shifted from intellectual/Marxist/dialectic politics to the realm of gender and sexual revolution that was more relevant when Los Bros were starting *Love and Rockets*. All of these characters have knowledge and political acumen, but they fail miserably in fulfilling their sexual desires and providing a narrative device with which nonintellectual Hispanics/Latinos can identify.[81]

For example, the role of Ofelia in Gilbert's flashback storyline *Poison River* perfectly presents the dichotomy between the ideals of social revolution and anarchist sexuality. At the time of its release, the longtime *Love and Rockets* reader knew Ofelia as the older, smart, and feisty Luba cousin who rambles about politics but who has to take care of Luba's kids and swallow the results of Luba's chaotic love life and wild behavior. However, when we see them at an earlier stage in life in *Poison River*, Ofelia lives in another town, is a young revolutionary adamant about her political causes, and takes care of young Luba, who was abandoned by her father.

Ofelia is ambivalent about her political causes because she is a revolutionary and wants to help the oppressed but does not support the Communist government, which she sees as another dictatorship: "Yeah, yeah, I'm going even though it's gonna mostly be a bunch of extremist boneheads pathetically defending Stalin and his 'progressive' butchering . . ."[82] This is why she mocks her revolutionary comrades when they are burning an Eisenhower effigy, which looks more like Soviet prime minister Nikita Khrushchev.[83] However, Ofelia is also blinded to her own ideological flaws, which can be seen in several segments of the story. First, she displays racist attitudes against indigenous people, when she yells at young Luba for interacting with them because they are supposedly savages (an insinuation that they find insulting).[84] Second, her literary elitism separates her from the mass culture that Luba consumes, as seen with her complaints about the *Pedro Pacotilla* comic (a symbolic allusion to Yolanda Vargas Dulché's *Memín Pinguín*).[85]

The Pedro Pacotilla/Memín Pinguín role in *Poison River* is interesting because it was Gilbert's way of dealing with one of the recent controversies regarding Latino culture in the United States. *Memín Pinguín* is one of Mexico's most controversial comics because it is still very popular with many Mexican and Mexican American readers. Reprints continue to be sold in Mexican newsstands and in the U.S. Southwest, and in 2005, the Mexican government even issued a postal stamp featuring the character. Memín, however, is an Afro-Mexican character drawn with distorted racial features, similar to the "sambo" representation considered racist in contemporary United States culture.

Like her other comic, *María Isabel*, Yolanda Vargas Dulché's *Memín Pinguín* is an interesting soap opera/melodrama comic book that attempts to provide social commentary that fits postrevolutionary Mexican ideals. In my article "Coon Imagery in Will Eisner's *The Spirit* and Yolanda Vargas Duché's *Memín Pinguín* and Its Legacy in the Contemporary United States and Mexican Comic Book Industries," I attempted to explain the positive aspects of the narrative and why Mexican audiences still enjoy the comic, but I also explain in detail why it is racially offensive. One of the main problems is that Mundo Vid, the Mexican company that owns *Memín*, refuses to acknowledge that the drawings are racist and to include a warning label in the reprints. In addition, a lot of Mexican politicians have used the debates to promote Mexican nationalism by claiming they should not be lectured about race depictions by the United States.

Gilbert's parody of Memín was published before the controversy exploded in the United States in the mid-2000s, which shows the author was aware of the problems with the character, and he had attempted to criticize how Mexican and Latino mass audiences still consumed the character without being aware of its racist portrayal, as is the case of *María Isabel*, the other Vargas Dulché comic that I previously discussed. In *Poison River*, Gilbert self-reflexively, through one of Ofelia's Marxist friends, explains to American readers that characters such as Pedro Pacotilla (Memín's metaphor) have been criticized in Mexico by intellectuals and educators but "the little shit will outlive us all."[86]

Christopher Pizzino comments on Pedro/Memín's immortality in the following manner: "As images from Pedro comics recur throughout the years of Luba's life in 'Poison River,' it becomes obvious that Pedro never ages or changes; he represents comics driven by genre and ideology, unable or unwilling to protest an oppressive status quo. These kinds of comics contrast strongly with Gilbert's stories of *Palomar*, which allow for decay and transformation, and, at times, boldly critique social and political norms."[87] One of the elements that surprised me in my interview with Gilbert and Jaime is that they had not read the *Memín Pinguín* comics because they were written in Spanish. Therefore, Gilbert's critique is about the racist aesthetic of *Memín* and not about the themes featured in the book. In the interview I conducted with them, they say that they glanced at the comics when their older brother Mario brought them home and that they liked Sixto Valencia's art, even though they are critical of the Memín character. They could not read the Spanish text but certainly were self-aware of the racist visuals. It is almost as if Pedro Pacotilla/Memín Pinguín becomes an ambiguous symbol of how Latino artists may be resistant to the (from an American perspective) problematic aspects of their cultural heritage, even if they do not have full access to that heritage. To me this is very evident in how throughout *Poison River* Gilbert juxtaposes images of Pedro Pacotilla with the violence and betrayals that marked Luba's and Ofelia's life experiences. It is nefarious imagery of memories that still remain, just like the *Memín* comic, and it subverts the idealization of Mexican culture and aesthetics sought by the Chicano movement in the 1960s, especially in terms of racial representation. In that sense, Pedro Pacotilla's *Memín* parody is an important departure from the precepts of the Chicano/Latino movement, particularly the latter's embrace of an imaginary Latin American *mestizaje* devoid of racial problems.

Mexican intellectuals resent the success of Pedro Pacotilla. Gilbert Hernandez, *Beyond Palomar*, 36. © Gilbert Hernandez.

At the end of the first *Love and Rockets* volume, Gilbert moved Pipo and Luba's family to the United States. At first I thought it was a natural move the artist had made to show readers how characters evolve on the transnational stage. I gave political meaning to the shift, although in my interview Gilbert assured me that his intentions were purely related to no longer being able to produce stories in a small-town setting. He needed to move the characters to a metropolis in order to reenergize his *Palomar* universe. However, as the storylines now feature more U.S. Latino characters such as Fritz and Venus, I feel that the narratives are closer to his own reality, as they feature a new type of Latino "geek" intellectual that follows postmodern traditions and that is influenced more by popular culture than the literary canon that Palomar intellectuals constantly tried to imprint upon the younger generations.

Fritz's Movies and the Unreliability of the Ethnic Text in the United States

The Palomar intellectuals' inefficiency in providing an alternative narrative that empowered the community and dealt with their own sexual neurosis subtly led to the current "geek" phase in the *Palomar* saga. Even though Luba had lost her love for Pedro Pacotilla comics, she had run Palomar's movie theater and she brought in all types of B movies, such as Bruce Lee's martial arts films. Her initiative allowed the people of Palomar to be in contact with mass culture, something derided by traditional intellectuals. However, despite the access to popular culture that Luba provides to the people, she also limits them to becoming consumers who do not engage in artistic work and thus can never tell of their own experiences to the rest of the world.

This situation is challenged with the arrival of Howard, an American photographer, to the town of Palomar. At first he interacts well with the locals, who are excited about his taking photos and publishing them in a global American magazine. However, he is mostly interested in the exotic aspects of the town, and this creates a conflict with Luba's family. He initially wants to take a photo of them in front of their "third world cinema" but is annoyed when he sees that Luba and her family dress up for the pictures, for he wanted a more "native" look that enhanced the poverty traits of the town. Initially, many of the Palomar residents resent the intentions of the American photographer, but ironically the intellectual Heraclio and Israel, an economically successful character, support the idea because they say that even if it is through exoticism, this will be the only way that people from around the world will know that Palomar exists.[88]

Toward the end of the first volume of *Love and Rockets*, Gilbert decided to move the story to the United States and reunite Luba's Palomar family with her half sisters Fritz and Petra. In the United States, Luba's neighbor Pipo becomes a successful entrepreneur and the sometimes lover and producer of Fritz (Luba's half sister), who stars in a series of B movies. These B movies are Gilbert's original graphic novels, such as *Chance in Hell, The Troublemakers, Love from the Shadows*, and *Maria M*, Book 1 and 2. Other movies appear in fake posters and seem to be based on short segments published in *Love and Rockets*. When reading these stories, one engages in an interesting metaexperience, as these movies/graphic novels recreate Fritz's career and her fictional roles, from being an extra in *Chance in Hell*, to a secondary character in *The Troublemakers*, and finally a protagonist in *Love from the Shadows* and *Maria M*.

This metafictional representation has reached its peak with the project

Maria M, in which Fritz stars as her mother *Maria* and Fritz's niece Doralis (Luba's daughter) writes the screenplay based on the events of *Poison River*. Doralis merges characters and storylines in a way that *Love and Rockets* did not, yet readers would recognize the events from the earlier work in a bizarre Gilbert intertextuality. The reason this segment of the *Palomar* story is important is that it shows how the characters are finally able to construct their own narrative reality once they gain economic power and indulge freely in sexuality, something that the intellectual revolution in Palomar's past could not achieve.

The character of Fritz is at the epicenter of this empowerment, but she could be interpreted as a controversial figure because the story could be read as a male comic fan fantasy if the reader does not pay attention to some of the details that Gilbert provides. For example, Fritz has inherited her mother's and Luba's voluptuous body and she also enjoys her sexuality. At times, Gilbert portrays too many scenes of Fritz's sexual life, which occasionally crosses the line into pornography. However, the character is smart, educated (she holds a psychology degree), and a well-read science fiction fan. This makes her also very sympathetic, especially since she performs entertaining roles in B-movie genre narratives. Her background and the integration of sexuality into her discourse make her a new type of intellectual and situate her outside of the elitist and academic literary circles from the past, of which Heraclio and Ofelia were part.

At some point in the story, Fritz abandons her job as a psychologist to become the sexualized star of B movies. However, her stardom allows her, together with her writer Doralis and her producer Pipo, to write in her own way a different aspect of the Latino experience through the bizarre crime, fantasy, science fiction, and other surrealist genres in which she chooses to involve herself. By doing this, she continues and succeeds in what was started with the original Chicano and Latino movements, the ability of the Latino/Hispanic ethnicity to be able to interact with the Anglophone narrative while incorporating its own experience.

These Fritz B-movie graphic novel adaptations have baffled fans, readers, and critics because they do not add a linear plot or explicit character development to the saga. Academics have certainly tried to find a logical meaning to the stories by providing formalistic and ideological points to the readers. For example, F. Vance Neill states that in these stories "Gilbert Hernandez presents his argument criticizing European-American culture via the implied author of his narratives, the visual rhetoric of the image-text relationship, and the tacit ethic of living that circulate amongst the characters."[89] On the other hand, Frederick Aldama discusses the role of mood in helping the reader unlock the noir genre tools that make the stories understandable, and the implied deconstruction of gender issues.[90]

Many of these academic interpretations are excellently stated and, as I discussed in chapter 1, may provide for better explanations than what the author intended with these intertextual self-adaptations of his own material. I think what makes Gilbert's meta-approach interesting is something very simple with which he redefines the Latino ethnic narrative and comic books. By making the *Love and Rockets* reader (Latino or not Latino) aware of the possible ambiguity and artificiality of the ethnic narrative, it places the Chicano/Latino narrative on the same level of other Anglophone narratives as it displays the idea of performativity. It shows that the conventions have moved from the Marxist/revolutionary/anti-hegemonic/ethnic building tradition (which is still relevant in many cases) about constructing the self into the more ambivalent postmodernism that already understands how the narrative structures function. Critics such as Aldama have noted the evolution in complexity of the Latino comic book narrative:

> Indeed, the evolved capacity to employ increasingly more sophisticated symbolic modes of representation in narrative allowed for more complex orchestrations of temporality and eventually led to the splitting of narrative into a double chronologic: the way the story is told (third person, say) and the content of the story (the events and characters, say). This helps us understand better why a Latino comic book author-artist can manipulate narrative point of view, lighting, panel layout, and so on not only to tell a story, but also to engage audiences and readers on a number of different levels.
>
> In reading the signposts laid out by Latino comic book and comic strip author-artists, we are cued to reexperience or reconstruct our core selves in complex and specifically directed ways: ways that direct us to realize a fuller experience of U.S. ethnicity—specifically, Latino and Latina identity. All this while constantly reminding us of the difference between self and life, and life and fiction.[91]

In a broader sense, scholar Chela Sandoval explores the theoretical implications of converging political activism and the new postmodern age (often accused of not being political enough) into what postcolonial theory calls the Third Space. In her book *Methodology of the Oppressed*, she provides a comprehensive analysis of intertextual and postmodern ideas and tries to make sense of the historical contradictions, concluding:

Indeed, my argument is that it is the ability to conceive of the equal-rights, revolutionary, supremacist, and separatist ideologies as constructed by the oppressed in liberatory action, to understand them as forms of consciousness that are themselves readable, inhabitable, interpretable, and transformable when necessary, and to recognize their structural relations to one another through an overgirding theory and method of oppositional consciousness, that comprises the fifth and differentially acting form of consciousness and activity in opposition. The differential form of oppositional consciousness is both another mode of these oppositional ideologies and at the same time a transcendence of them.[92]

The representation of Fritz is a reflection of this new, more complex type of identity of the oppressed, and its new, more complex artistic depiction. More importantly, the B-movie graphic novels become a *mise en abyme* of sorts, where Fritz mirrors Gilbert and in turn is mirrored by the protagonist in her own narratives. Both Fritz and Gilbert depict a complex identity that has moved beyond the binaries established at the onset of the Chicano movement. In addition, they are both freed from the shackles of dogmatic traditions and have transcended the prudishness against sexuality in the United States as well as of their Hispanic culture of origin. This process has taken over thirty years and includes the appropriation of both the concepts of the Latin American town (Palomar) and the United States (Fritz and Luba's adventures in the United States) into a new vision that is performed by Gilbert's characters.

Maggie's Genre Constructions: From Her Punk Sci-Fi Fetish and Political Adventures to Just Surviving Adult Life Melodrama

Jaime's *Locas* saga differs from Gilbert's *Palomar* storyline in its more prominent use of fantastic elements. As the main plot has become more centered on Maggie's melodramatic life, the appearance of genre in the series signals emotional phases in the characters that may also represent the moods of the comic creator at the time. For example, the early sci-fi "Mechanics" phase where Maggie lives in a sci-fi world represents a deconstructivist phase influenced by Jaime's punk days and is clearly an attempt on the author's part to parody or re-envision the genres promoted by the American comic book industry at the time. Still, some of the secondary characters such as Penny Century and Rena Titañón remain involved in larger-than-life genre plots as opposed to Maggie's down-to-earth melodrama, which in a way becomes a representation of how the industry narratives, different genres, and ethnic consciousness are interconnected within different levels of realism.

When scholar Frederick Aldama asked him about the saga's shift into realism (which some comic book fans regret), Jaime responded that they wanted to get into the gritty emotional stuff and the dinosaurs were getting in the way.[93] Gilbert obviously made this shift to a more down-to-earth (but still bizarre) melodrama earlier in his *Palomar* saga (after the outlandishness of "BEM"), but both brothers have occasionally returned to their genre roots. Gilbert has done it through his graphic novels about Fritz's movies and his recent *Palomar* flashback that was told in his miniseries *New Tales of Old Palomar* (reprinted as *Children of Palomar*). Jaime occasionally has done the same with the recent Penny Century superhero arc that I discussed in chapter 1. In a way, Gilbert's Fritz movies (graphic novels) and Jaime's incursions into the fantastic and the bizarre, while subverting gender and genre tropes, represent the "punk" intertextual defiance employed by the Chicano/a punk performers, as Habell-Pallán described.

One could say that the main storyline in Jaime's *Locas* is the growth of Maggie into adulthood and the fluid evolution of her love life. In the early sci-fi punk segments, she is linked romantically to Rand Race, who is a parody of comic book heroic masculinity in the fantastic period of the serial. She then proceeds to have a lesbian affair with Hopey during the punk phase of the character until their relationship is dissolved. In the later part of her life, as presented in recent *Love and Rockets* stories, she is dating the character of Ray Dominguez, but this relationship could change course as Jaime continues to develop Maggie into her mature adult phase. Jaime has drawn the character differently in each phase of life and has made her look chubbier as she grows older. Some fans have wished that she stayed young forever (as most comic characters do in the United States), but Jaime feels that these visual changes help the reader to perceive her in a more realistic manner, as the development of adult emotions are also tied to the body. In an interview with Solvej Schou for *Entertainment Weekly*, Jaime said the following: "Me getting older helps me write my characters getting older. Aging the characters make them more human to me. The older they get, the more human they get. I only have so many stories I can tell, especially for the last 30 years. Maggie at 17, and Maggie at 45, will make a story seem different. I can put them in the same situation, but they'll be different. The aging makes it keep it fresh somehow. I've been a fan of comics and comic strips where they never age, like the Peanuts characters, and that was fine."[94]

The lesbian phase of Maggie and Hopey's lives was important for the queer movements in the 1980s, as it portrayed Latina characters in a non-heterosexual masculine-centered setting. This was compatible with some of the gender goals of Chicano punk performance, as Michelle Habell-Pallán describes in her book *Loca Motion*. She writes in particular about Alfaro's performance:

> Alfaro's performance pieces help to invent a new Chicano (a) subject whose identity is not necessarily based on the ideology of static Chicano cultural nationalism, which posits an essential Chicano subject (always hetero-sexual), but instead is based on a subtle understanding of how cultural identity and identification is in constant flux. This new Chicano (a) subject is rooted in Chicano culture, but, unlike cultural nationalists, it is also committed to the politics of anti-homophobia, and anti-sexism. He or she resists and changes dominant inscriptions of ethnic identity and dominant structuring of social relations.[95]

One of the narrative elements that has been praised about Maggie's character is her sexual fluidity that does not define her as either heterosexual or homosexual. Scholar Esther Saxey states that Jaime's shifting portrayal of the character's sexual desires avoided the closure of "coming out" storylines that abounded in gay literature where the characters had to be sexually defined one way or another. In a way, Jaime's refusal to commit to a genre, realism, and defined sexuality is what makes his *Locas* narrative representative of a truly postmodern ethnic literature. Saxey adds: "These ambiguities of identity/narrative are supported by techniques that Hernandez employs for unsettling closure and end-determined narrative in his strips. Readers already wait a month or two months for each comic. But it is perfectly possible for an artist to condense a traditional plot of closure into one issue, or provide a longer story arc over several issues. Instead, in Love and Rockets, this underlying delay is enhanced by further evasions of closure."[96]

Since the beginning of the *Locas* saga, Jaime had expressed to the readers that his characters lived in different realities even though they shared a Latino heritage. At the end of the story "Maggie vs. Maniakk," Jaime's last panel is one of the best representations of Bakhtin's dialogism as he visualizes the three genres in which Maggie, Penny, and Hopey think they belong. Maggie dreams of being the love interest of a superhero, Penny pictures herself as a superheroine who bullies an alien life form, while Hopey sees herself as the intellectual inquisition (as befitting someone with punk ideals) who metaphorically executes both Penny and Maggie for being airheads and wanting to fulfill the genre structures they wish to embody.[97]

It is important here to discuss the most influential persons in Maggie's life in order to understand how they represent the intertextual genre connections

Maggie, Penny, and Hopey visualize the respective genres to which they belong. Jaime Hernandez, *Maggie the Mechanic*, 98. © Jamie Hernandez.

of fully realized bicultural Latinas. First, as explained in the first chapter, Maggie's friend Penny Century represents the desire to enter and disrupt the Anglophone culture that for a long period of time had isolated Latinos from participating in pop culture. Rena Tintañón represents through her wrestling profession and political adventures the Latino political iconography of the Chicano resistance movement. Hopey symbolizes the punk movement that no longer exists for Jaime and Gilbert but that was essential in forming their adult worldviews.

It is difficult to explain the development of these characters in a linear way, as Jaime usually rewrites them through flashbacks and through the perceptions of other characters. For example, Penny Century is glamorous at the beginning of the story, but several issues later her flashbacks display her humble origins as part of a very poor family.[98] Rena is presented as an invincible wrestler and freedom fighter, but later some characters question the validity of her alleged heroics, and some flashbacks further affect our perception of her character.[99] Hopey is the coolest Latina punk character that exists, but Jaime certainly presents also her flaws and complexes throughout the *Locas* story through memories and other narrative devices.

As Penny and her superhero obsessions represent the predominant genre trend in Anglophone comics, the Latino narrative and its political implications is represented by her mentor Rena Titañón.[100] Rena, who is introduced in the second issue of the first volume of *Love and Rockets* in the story "Mechanics," is a champion professional female wrestler and the nemesis of Maggie's aunt Vicki, who plays the role of the heel in the wrestling circuits. Wrestling is a performance sport that is popular on both sides of the U.S.-Mexico border and is generally associated with masculinity. However, just like he did with "The Return of the Ti-Girls," Jaime features predominantly Latino and Latin American female wrestlers in *Locas*, thus making it a woman-centric narrative.

Maggie is not athletically gifted, which is why she is not interested in fulfilling the family wrestling tradition started by her aunt Vicki. However, she is attracted to her aunt's nemesis Rena because of her larger-than-life mythology that involves being a former champion in the United States, as well as being a hero of the people and freedom fighter. As an American Latina, Maggie is not necessarily the most political person, as she is more worried about things like love, and she certainly stumbles when sharing political adventures with Rena abroad. In a way, Jaime parodies the U.S. Latino movement's utopian ideas that every ethnic group is political because they are not part of the ruling hegemony. Rena has the know-how to affect change due to her former guerilla experiences, but Maggie is completely clueless to the political realities of the world for much of the time.

After introducing the characters in several issues and segments, Jaime brings these political issues to the front in the famous "Mechanics" story. Maggie goes to a fictional country (Zimbodia), where she is to work with Rand Race, the object of her affection, on fixing a spaceship that has landed in the jungle. In this story, Jaime does not follow the traditional layout of a comic-book page/narrative. He draws the events but excludes all dialogue, and instead superimposes Maggie's letters to Hopey. At times, he interrupts this layout to incorporate traditional panels that show Hopey's reaction to the letters.

Maggie's letters sound like the words of a colonizing invader employed by a corporation, and her perspective in the letter replicates the dominant Euro-centric discourse that Hopey and therefore the reader can easily understand. Her descriptions of the natives are strange (as she claims they have big feet and olive skin), and Jaime enhances the portrayal of otherness by situating the plot in the jungle and adding dinosaurs into the mix.[101] Maggie displays very American-centric behavior, such as when she keeps trying to explain the foreign culture in her own Latino/Chicana terms (the natives' music as mariachi mixed with Corracobán music).[102] Even other Latina characters such as Penny Century participate in the sort of Orientalist perception of the third world, as she shows up half-naked (like the Jungle Girl character) at some point in the story hoping that the natives can give her superpowers.[103]

The story turns into a serious political adventure when Maggie discovers that the millionaire that hired them in reality plans to blow up the native village in order to make a profit.[104] Everything looks gloomy until Rena Titañón, the legendary wrestler, appears on the scene. Her background and origin are revealed, including how she lost her wrestling title, was kidnapped by a Zimbodian warlord, and as consequence became a rebel fighter. Because of her guerrilla experience, she knows the locals and their language, and through her, Maggie learns what is truly happening in the country from a Zimbodian perspective. Rena further helps Maggie escape danger, defeats the antagonists, and the bizarre colonial political adventure ends on a happy note.

In this storyline, Jaime parodies simultaneously Maggie's "gringa" ignorance and Hopey's punk political aloofness. While Maggie is being serious, Jaime ridicules her pessimism as he juxtaposes her narration with Hopey and her friends buying drugs or reading the letters while getting drunk in the safety of the United States. When Maggie survives dangerous events such as a tropical disease, Jaime mocks her perception of tropicalism, as she assumes what defeated the disease was her mestiza Chicana blood.[105] On the other hand, Hopey's anarchism is also parodied, as she does not care about Maggie's experiences and is mostly worried about being perceived as committed to a cause. An example of this is when Maggie says she is working for the government and apologizes to Hopey because she is antigovernment, but then she rethinks her statement and says that she is probably anti-antigovernment.

By making fun of both of his main characters in different ways, Jaime actually builds up Rena as the political heroine from the past that represents modernity and helps the progressive movements that championed equality.

However, not everything Jaime discloses to the reader about Rena is complimentary. For example, when we see her story from Maggie's aunt Vicki's point of view, it is revealed that the cause for the latter's resentment is that she was stuck in the role of an antagonist in order to sell Rena's heroism. In addition, Vicki constantly gets annoyed by the mythology built around Rena's revolutionary persona. Vicki explains that Rena left wrestling because she was pregnant and not because, as the official story goes, she was kidnapped by a warlord (and the truth falls in between according to multiple points of view).[106] Rena also has a problematic relationship with her son, as he has been raised by one of her male wrestler friends and Rena's guerrilla warfare abroad has not allowed them to form a close relationship.

The role of motherhood is important in Jaime's stories because it is an issue that affects both Rena and Penny Century in the fulfillment of their dreams as heroines, even though they function within different genres. In Penny Century's last adventure, the character embraces her mature age and establishes a closer connection to her daughters when she forgets about her silly obsessions with superheroes. This may seem like a patronizing fantasy about motherhood, but Jaime clearly establishes that it does not work in the same manner for every woman. For example, Angel (one of Maggie's friends) also forgets her superheroine obsession, even though she has no children.[107]

The main difference between Penny Century and Rena Titañón as Maggie's friends and representatives of other genres that Maggie could have followed (the fantastic and the political) is that Penny does not age (like Pedro Pacotilla in Gilbert's *Poison River*) because she belongs to the culture industry that remains the same and that is not realistic, while Rena does because she belongs to a narrative that is situated closer to reality. Maggie has that realization about Penny in Jaime's *God and Science: Return of the Ti-Girls*, specifically when the character says goodbye to her as she leaves Penny in her eternal comic book reality and goes back to her comic book reader dimension. On the other hand, Jaime shocks Maggie and the reader when he brings back the now much older character of Rena in the *La Maggie La Loca* serial that he ran in the *New York Times*.

This particular project works as a stand-alone storyline, but it is a much more gratifying experience for a longtime *Love and Rockets* fan. Jaime recreates the visual structure (no word balloons to express dialogue) of the original "Mechanics" story, but this time narrated from a middle-aged Maggie's point of view. The more mature Maggie also has a more mature perspective in life and tells the story about her trip to a remote island to visit an older Rena. Maggie is shocked to see how Rena has aged, as she is a mythological figure for the Latin American characters.

During her visit, Maggie is happy to see Rena but becomes bored, as the old woman is trying to relive her past at her old age. Rena continues to teach wrestling, flees the local market in paranoid fear of assassins, and watches videos of her old wrestling matches.[108] At some point Maggie has an argument with her, goes out to sea, and barely survives a boating accident. On her return, she finds out that Rena was arrested for attacking two people in the town, but she is quickly released under the pressure of a vigil organized by the locals in front of the police station. When Rena comes out of the holding cell, she is received as a heroine by the people. Maggie finally realizes that Rena also has Penny Century's immortality but in a different, more spiritual way. Rena will age physically, but will remain an ever-young symbol of the ideology of revolution that will always be alive in us.[109]

The most interesting element of the *Locas* saga is how Jaime has created a pastiche where the narrative does not commit to either form, ideology, or sexuality. Even though the saga's reality is mostly filtered through Maggie's perspective, Jaime is able to portray how the narrative is shaped by a shared experience that does not value one perspective over the other. The reader may identify with Maggie's more mundane stories but admire the outlandish goals of both Penny Century and Rena Titañón, who are superior and inferior to Maggie in several ways. Maggie's ordinariness helps us understand Penny and Rena, and vice versa. The way in which the characters, genre, ideology, and form are interconnected to provide the reader with a dialogical reality is what places Jaime's comics among the most inspired in the history of the United States.[110]

Conclusion

Both Gilbert's and Jaime's storylines benefit from their serial aspects, as their characters grow with the creators. Their original stories represented the anarchic punk attitudes of their youth as they played with genres to defy the conventions of how Latinos were represented in the media. I have shown how their narratives initially subverted the comics that were published in the American mainstream industry but also defied the antagonistic Chicano/Latino narratives from the 1960s that saw identity as the rejection of American values. Both brothers see themselves as part of the United States, yet are proud of their Mexican heritage and community that allow them to depict their realities in a different way. Their pastiche narratives proudly display a bicultural intertextuality that modifies hegemony through a self-referential postmodernity that reinvents the American narrative and contributes to the perception of Latino narratives as an equal to traditional Anglophone narratives.

When discussing the politics of the postmodern narrative, Linda Hutcheon draws a conclusion that also applies quite well to the works of Gilbert and Jaime Hernandez:

> In saying this, I realize that I am going against a dominant trend in contemporary criticism that asserts that the postmodern is disqualified from political involvement because of its narcissistic and ironic appropriation of existing images and stories and its seemingly limited accessibility—to those who recognize the sources of parodic appropriation and understand the theory that motivates it. But, what this study of the forms and politics of postmodern representation aims to show is that such a stand is probably politically naive and, in fact, quite impossible to take in the actual art of postmodernism. Postmodern art cannot but be political, at least in the sense that its representations—its images and stories—are anything but neutral, however "aestheticized" they may appear to be in their parodic self-reflexivity. While the postmodern has no effective theory of agency that enables a move into political action, it does work to turn its inevitable ideological grounding into a site of de-naturalizing critique.[111]

The main difference between Gilbert and Jaime's pastiche approach in their respective sagas is how they perceive the otherness of their own heritage. Gilbert attempts to create a transnational space with the town of Palomar, but by excluding the political institutions and dialectic clashes of modernist narratives, this imaginary transnational space becomes more of a metaphor for transnational identity. *Palomar* is a representative of an ethnic imaginary that is mostly about the author's own condition as part of an ethnic group that did not have too much of a voice in the United States until recently. Palomar's disconnect from the rest of the world to me embodies the isolation that Chicano communities had (and may still have). As Gilbert's characters developed and became stronger, they created their own narratives (Fritz's movies), which are not necessarily political in nature but that do achieve the dream where ethnicities can play with genres in the same way that people with access to hegemonic culture do.

Jaime approaches the issue in a different way. Since the beginning of his *Locas* saga, the characters broke into the other comic book genres as they became possible models that Maggie may follow. Through Maggie, who represents Jaime's own development as an adult, the author depicts how the comic book industry confines the characters into predetermined narrative strains. Penny Century represents the superheroes that are mainstream, Rena symbolizes the Latino/wrestling/political heritage, and Hopey, the alternative comics brand with which *Love and Rockets* was launched. Maggie has a fallout with the three characters at several points in the story but, as she matures, she realizes that they all embody Latino culture in different ways (the hegemonic, the political, and the anarchist) and that they all contribute to a new world where the Latinos have the ability to form or embrace a distinct identity within the umbrella of "latinidad."

The *Love and Rockets* project is the most astonishing ethnic comic book that has been published in the United States, and its model will be very difficult to replicate. The saga is difficult to understand due to its complex plotlines, its multitude of characters, and its intricate intertextuality. Yet it has achieved great popularity and an almost legendary status among many readers, in addition to prompting a plethora of critical work. That is why I am confident that the academic study of this project, as well as of the Hernandez Brothers' work in general, will flourish and that *Love and Rockets* will become one of the models to follow in the future, especially in terms of ethnic representation. It is truly a foundational narrative in both Latino and Anglophone culture, a groundbreaking work rooted in the U.S. comix tradition, yet providing a fresh reconceptualization of gender, sexuality, and latinidad.

spotlight 3

"Chiro the Indian" (from *Love and Rockets: New Stories #1*, vol. 1)

IN CHAPTER 2, I discussed the similarities and differences between Rius's depiction of a fictional small Mexican town (San Garabato in *Los superma-chos*) and Gilbert's trans-Latin vision in his fictional Palomar. One of the stories that made me examine these connections in detail was Gilbert's "Chiro the Indian," a recent collaboration with his older brother Mario in the latest volume of *Love and Rockets*. Mario, as the older brother, was the one who actually brought Mexican comics into the Hernandez's household and was thus more aware of their distinctive national aesthetics. "Chiro the Indian" is not necessarily the most acclaimed segment drawn by Gilbert, but it is one of the best in recreating Rius's aesthetics and cultural values. Still, there are a few differences that shift the story away from being a political comic, as the parody changes from criticizing hegemony to disrupting the revolutionary goal of the story itself. This is achieved by means of the surrealistic ending that is very ambivalent about whether the subversive politics of the story can topple hegemony.

The story is only six pages long, due to space constraints during the release of the *Love and Rockets* relaunch, but it includes a lot of material to analyze. The main indigenous character is named Chiro, and his family consists of his wife Preciosa and his daughter Moom-Fah. They are portrayed as an indigenous family, but Mario and Gilbert do not disclose in which Latin American nation-state they reside and are oppressed. This is the comic closest to Rius's *Los supermachos* that Gilbert has produced because Chiro and his relatives are the victims of all the components of Latin American hegemony, including the army, the Catholic Church, and the aristocracy. The main plot revolves around the rich couple of señor Feo (Mr. Ugly) and señora Maldita (Mrs. Cursed), who want to scare Chiro and Preciosa through the use of religious beliefs (both Christian and Aztec) in order to acquire a plot of land that was deeded in perpetuity to the indigenous couple.[1]

In "Chiro the Indian," Gilbert's art is more cartoony than how he usually draws the *Palomar* saga, and it is used more for laughs than for emotional drama. The characters are purposefully not developed emotionally, and they are simply political chess pieces like the ones Rius created in his comics. Mario and Gilbert's parody criticizes the role of religion in oppressing the indigenous communities and how it is used by the Latin American (perhaps Mexican) government as an excuse to isolate these communities. A fake Virgin and Quetzalcoatl apparitions enacted by the rich couple make Preciosa and Chiro act strangely in town, which in the end justifies Chiro's exile into the isolated Indian communities that lack European values.[2] All of these elements would fit Rius's comics with the exception of the supernatural ending that the Mexican author's Marxist leanings would not condone.

At the end of the story, the other indigenous characters bring to town the god Quetzalcoatl, who lives (among humans) nearby. He sees how the rich people have taken advantage of Chiro and his family and burns them all to death, thus sacrificing them. As a result of the sacrifice, rain finally comes into the town, and Chiro exclaims, "At least my false idol brought rain."[3] From a political point of view, Mario and Gilbert destroy the hegemonic Eurocentric antagonists through Quetzalcoatl's fury, but by achieving this through supernatural prowess instead of revolution, they fail to provide a pragmatic solution to the plight of the oppressed, something sought by the revolutionary traditions. However, there is still ideological content in this Latino/Chicano narrative, as the indigenous mythology is the one that achieves victory at the end and not the Eurocentric traditions that dominate both the Latin American right and left.

chapter three

Interview with
Jaime and Gilbert Hernandez

IN NOVEMBER 2013, I went to Ohio State University to attend the Billy Ireland Cartoon Library & Museum's Grand Opening Festival of Cartoon Art. Professor Frederick Aldama was able to arrange a one-hour interview for me with Gilbert and Jaime Hernandez. Their conversation with professor Christopher González was the keynote event for the festival and cosponsored by the Wexner Center for the Arts and Ohio State's University Office of Diversity and Inclusion. Later, I was also invited to join the brothers for dinner, which allowed me to talk to them in a more informal setting. This was a wonderful experience for me as a Los Bros Hernandez scholar and as a comic book fan.

To prepare for the interview, I read all the interviews I could find that Gilbert and Jaime Hernandez had given online, in the printed press, and in scholarly journals. I took notes on what types of questions they had already answered before (to avoid repetition). In my opinion, the best interviews they have given are the ones collected in the *Love and Rockets Companion*, published by Fantagraphics and conducted by Gary Groth and Neil Gaiman. Still, there are great nuggets of knowledge that appear in several others, which I have quoted throughout my manuscript and which are referenced in the bibliography.

My main goal with this interview was to discuss certain themes that I explore in the book, such as the role of the history of the American comic book industry and distribution in the Hernandez brothers' careers, how they perceive the "Latinness" of their comics, and how the queer/sexual content of their books affect the reception of their work. I edited the conversation by topics instead of chronology to give the written piece a more solid narrative structure, which should help the reader understand the issues in a more clear manner.

My biggest discovery was that both Gilbert and Jaime are still fans of comic book culture and its genres. While conducting my research, I never questioned the fact that they are comic book fans, since their intertextual narrative devices are so complex. However, because sometimes their stories are so critical of and cynical about the more simplistic and traditionalist traits of the American comic book industry, I felt that perhaps they were not as wide-eyed as other comic book creators who only dabble in superhero narratives and do not challenge the industry. Yet at our dinner together, they were discussing all types of recent comic book folklore, including films such as *Thor: The Dark World* and *Pacific Rim*, and even more obscure subjects such as Kevin Smith's television show *Comic Book Men*. They were certainly as hardcore as comic book fans can be, and I enjoyed discovering that they are not only legendary artists but also voracious readers and lovers of the comic book medium.

On the Evolution of the American Comic Book Industry and Issues of Distribution

Enrique García (EG): Thank you for agreeing to share your thoughts on some of the topics that I think might be of interest to the readers of this book. Earlier you talked to some Ohio State faculty and students over lunch, and one of the Latina graduate students mentioned that she was not able to read your comics when she was growing up because of their adult content. At the comic book store, she was instead encouraged to read superhero material, such as *Catwoman*, which was supposedly better suited for children. This relationship between readership and retail space was depicted in one of your *Love and Rockets* stories when the character of Venus is not able to buy *Grip*, one of Gilbert's comics in a record store because she is too young, and instead she is directed to the traditional comic book store to purchase the superhero stories she hates. This particular scene portrayed the alternative stores as the physical space where your comics are featured.

Gilbert Hernandez (GH): Right. What is interesting is that at the time, I just liked the title of *Grip*, so I put it in there before I actually published it. In the Venus story, *Grip* is actually a porn title. The character is too young to understand it and finds it disgusting, because she has never seen something like it before.

EG: I found interesting your take on American comic book distribution in this story, because it reflected my own experience with Los Bros' comics. While I was living in Puerto Rico, my superhero-centered stores didn't carry your books, so it wasn't until I went to grad school at UMASS Amherst that I read *Poison River* in one of my graduate classes, and I was later able to acquire your works in alternative record store chains such as Newbury Comics, where both of you were featured as stars.

GH: It's funny, we were talking earlier about getting an award in Beverly Hills with lots of fancy people, and then you go to the local comic books store and our books are all the way in the back. Many people tell me that when they go to their local comic book stores, most of our work is usually located in the porn section. To this day, thirty years after we began *Love and Rockets*. However, the bookstores in Beverly Hills will have them in the front and display them proudly.

Jaime Hernandez (JH): In my comic store, our comic is in one of the back shelves with the archival collections.

GH: That is weird. Because it is new material.

JH: So there will be a giant *Sandman* box set next to it. I guess it's selling now and they think it's the same clientele.

GH: But it is different [from *Sandman*].

EG: One of the topics I discuss in the first segment of my book is about the comic book industry because I think that the way it is set up has an effect on distribution. When I teach comics in the classroom, I have a feeling that students do not have the historical knowledge to understand how institutions such as the Comics Code came to be, how the underground comix from the '60s defied this unique censorship system through distribution in what we would call with affection "hippie stores," and how *Love and Rockets* continues the legacy of this movement in its own manner. This is important to know because it is key to understanding how *Love and Rockets* functions as a comic.

GH: You are right. Now we have a bunch of young readers that began reading comics in the 1980s and '90s and, like you said, they don't know the history of the industry.

EG: Most of my students actually have barely read any comics at all, so when I ask them what they have read, most of their answers are *Calvin and Hobbes*. Most readers may not even be aware of modern comic book culture either.

GH and JH: Right.

EG: I always thought the problem in the U.S. is that we have censorship, but it is an economic one that does not come officially from the government. The Comics Code did not ban anything, but it made it hard for the alternative comics to exist and have decent distribution. Even though the direct comics market kind of helped in the early '80s, that market is dominated by Marvel and DC. It's not official government censorship, but it crushed a lot of the other smaller companies.

JH: Yes, I was astonished when I found out that the original Comics Code was formed when some comic book publishers established a pact. Does that mean that EC could have still published its own stuff?

GH: The Senate hearings hurt them because stores would not carry them anymore, you know, the grocery stores. Yes, I think they would not have gotten distribution at the end.

EG: They could publish them but could not put their product out there.

GH: Which is why their stories turned to piracy plots, *Impact*, etc.

JH: Which is why Warren [the company] published magazines instead.

GH: Which is why *Mad* turned into a magazine. Kurtzman and all of these guys said, "We can't change *Mad*." They wanted to clean up *Mad*, too! Which was a kids' comic too. For some reason they thought if it was a magazine and in black and white, kids would not look at them. Which, we found, was the truth.

JH: Yes, I remember finding them to be weird. When Mario would bring them, I was looking at the new magazine format and thinking, "This is weird, *Mad*."

EG: One of the things that my students do not understand is how the direct market also has its own manner of affecting distribution, even though it is no longer influenced by the Code. It is difficult for them to grasp the idea that comic book readers have to read a gigantic catalog [*Previews*], from which they have to order two months in advance. In addition, comic book store owners who do not see any interest in a title would not order any copy of it because he cannot return unsold copies to the publishing company. That is why I think that the new digital distribution is the future because the comics are available there any time that the customer wants, and they can buy every single issue of a series at any time. Further, any kid can buy your comics now on their tablet without their parents even knowing about it.

JH: Anyone can buy them?

EG: [laughing] Yes.

JH: I don't let my daughter read them yet!

EG: I think it helps independent creators with their distribution. So, do you think the readership situation is going to change with the new comic books applications for iPad, because they take your work out of the comic book store "ghetto"? Just last week I was in Vermont, in the middle of nowhere, buying your graphic novels in my tablet.

GH: True. Gary [Groth] just mentioned that. The last time I talked to him in a courtesy call, we were just chatting, and I asked if I can do a graphic novel for him. I was hinting to Fantagraphics, in the hope of making some extra money with a new hardcover. Then I hear a pause in the phone, and Gary says we are trying to get out of the comic book stores and look for alternative distribution venues (bookstores, alternative record stores, etc.). In comic book stores, *Love and Rockets* is always controversial, but everywhere else it's a good thing; in the comic world we are always pushed back.

In the traditional distribution, we are always behind *Batman* and *Superman*. Retailers would order superhero comics first, and those that have money left will take our comics after. Gary is very active trying to get past that and achieve new means of distribution systems.

EG: Do you think that digital distribution will affect how you create art?

GH: I am willing to go ahead and make comic books for the iPads but I will probably keep drawing on paper. [to Jaime] Remember when Brian Bolland found the perfect software to draw electronically but suddenly realized that there is no original art, and he makes a living selling original art. So he went back to paper; I guess he does both at the same time.

On the Financial Support from Readers

EG: It seems to me that the buying habits of a *Love and Rockets* reader and those of a *Spider-Man* reader are not very different. Both help the titles keep afloat by buying the new issues, and cannot wait to buy the same material in hardcovers, trades, etc.

GH: We appreciate the serial nature of the narrative, in which a cliff-hanger would make you come back, which is what we liked in *Spider-Man*, *Archie*, and others. We are just making versions of the same comics we read as kids, but for adults.

EG: But you need also this loyalty from the reader, because even powerhouses like Marvel and DC need their monthly sales. If their readers just wait for the collections, many of the titles get canceled. So *Love and Rockets* also needs the traditional comic book fans, the alternative readers, and the academics to buy the serial version of the title to keep you afloat.

GH: Yes. At some point there was a problem, because many like to read our books in the collections they find in libraries, and they would not bother with the magazine at all. I would ask them, "Wait, you wait three years to read *Love and Rockets*?" Then they realize they could read it every few months.

EG: I don't think they realize the importance of buying the serial version. I see all the time the writers of DC's *Vertigo* line pleading with the readers to buy the monthlies because they are afraid that their titles will be canceled. At some point the reader has to have faith in the author's work and subscribe to the title in the comic book store, assuming that its quality is going to remain good.

GH: We are conscious of that. We never want to betray the audience, and would love to always fulfill their expectations because we don't want them to stop, and we would love for them to continue with us even though they have to take that chance with the subscription.

On Intertextual Connections and How Different Readers Perceive Their Work

EG: In another interview, you said that at a convention, a comic book fan dismissed *Love and Rockets* as a soap. I was wondering if that was because the fan was reading a Latino text. However, Latin soap operas are short, last only one season, and have an ending. Or it might have been because your work reminded him of the American soaps that are on at 2 p.m.?

GH: Well, I always practically say that when it's like a soap, it's because it's about girls and their feelings and not about superheroes, even though all the elements of the soap opera are in the superhero stories. I think it was Charles Hatfield who brought up the fact that Stan Lee based the Marvel Universe on the romance genre.

JH: It's obvious in *Spider-Man*.

GH: If you see all the continuity and all the way romance stories hook you in, it's very palpable in Marvel.

EG: John Romita used to draw romance comics before drawing *Spider-Man*.

GH: The reason *The Avengers* was so popular was the soap opera elements of connecting all the characters and plots together. However, when they use the term "soap opera," they use it with a negative connotation. Unfortunately, even in the indie scene where we are dealing with 90 percent boys, we are always asked why we have girls in our comics. My newest answer is that because there are more of them on the planet than men. They deserve at least half of the attention. They [some comic readers] don't care about women's feelings and they are immature.

EG: I have a more general question about your readership. Sometimes I feel comic book readers may understand some references to comic culture in your works, but they may not understand some of the more complex issues that academic specialists see in them (for example, references to Latino culture or to the punk scene in L.A.). At the same time, scholars may miss some other ethnic or comic book fan references, etc. Is there a perfect reader for your work?

GH: We gave up on the idea of wanting a specific reader. We would like them to be millionaires and buy a lot of copies, of course [smiles]. But their personalities and subcultures don't matter to us. Your readers usually gravitate toward what you have written, so whoever our readers are, whoever shows up to our signings, to our talks, etc. That's who bought our work, and we just enjoy this.

JH: I don't know if this is a good example, but I am sure *Tom Sawyer* has been printed in many different languages, and I always wondered how people deal with the backwoods language. Because everything is now spoon-fed to the audience, like Hollywood does. People have forgotten to work their way into the text to try to understand what is happening and then figure it out. It's like the young people who ask old couples, "How do you stay together after 50 years of matrimony," and the answer is you are supposed to work at it, but in this age you just get mad and run from the challenge. I don't want to digress too much, but what I mean is that some things take time to work for you.

On the Influence of Mexican Comics on Their Work

EG: Gilbert, one of the obscure cultural signifiers (to an American audience) that I encountered in your work is how you quote the character of Memín Pinguín (Pedro Pacotilla) in the *Poison River* storyline. This allusion/parody is important in the plot, but if the reader/comic book fan/scholar has not read the original, he/she may not understand what you are doing or what your goal is. They may mistake it as a parody of Ebony White, but to me it is obviously linked to the Mexican character. Did you read *Memín* as a kid?

GH: We had the comics at the house.

JH: Because Mario started buying them.

GH: And we liked the art.

Interview with Jaime and Gilbert Hernandez

EG: Did Mario read Mexican comics?

GH: Just for a little period. We didn't have that many. We got a couple of *El Santo* too. We liked the art with the little photographs.

EG: The reason I am asking too is because I read in previous interviews that your mother read comics too, and she introduced both of you to the medium. In *Poison River*, Luba reads the *Memín* type of comics (*Pedro Pacotilla*) so I was wondering if you were portraying her in some sort of way.

GH: I don't know. [to Jaime] Did Mom read Mexican comics?

JH: She watched a lot of Mexican movies for sure, but I don't know if she read Mexican comics. I think she was totally into American comics, which is what she had. I think she just told me recently that she read comics for the first time because some family member was in the army, and he brought back several comics, and she just looked at them and she said, "I want more of this." So she went to the store to look for more of them. I am guessing that the store was selling mostly American comics.

EG: In Puerto Rico, we had mostly Spanish translations of American comics, but in the 1980s they reprinted a lot of the older Mexican comics and sold them at the newsstands at a price much lower than that of the American comics. Thus, Puerto Ricans from my generation would be familiar with Mexican characters such as Kalimán, Memín, etc. I think they are still distributing Memín in the Southwest, which is still scandalous due to the new perceptions of race in contemporary American society.

GH: I never saw the Mexican postal stamps featuring Memín. [To Jaime] Remember? They never sold them in the United States because it is a racist character.

EG: This scandal is fascinating because many Mexicans do not perceive the character as racist. The son of Yolanda Vargas Dulché (*Memín*'s writer) told me how the ex-Mexican president Vicente Fox called him at midnight to complain that George W. Bush was criticizing him about the stamps. The Mexicans could not take a lesson of political correctness from Bush. [Gilbert and Jaime laugh] In *Poison River*, you portray the debates about the Mexican perception of the portrayal of race in comics, right?

GH: Yes, it was there but it was kind of superficial. I should have explored it in more detail. Something I hate in popular culture and movies is when they have a black topic, but there are no black characters to comment on the controversy. I did not have any black characters in *Poison River*, and I felt it was like the movie *Pleasantville*, where the subject was black people but you could not see any black characters discussing the situation, which makes me uncomfortable.

JH: Well, because it would be controversial to see the clash of white vs. black.

EG: Another question I have regarding *Memín* and the Mexican comics influences is about one of your recent shorts titled "Chiro the Indian."

GH: [To Jaime] Was it yours?

JH: It was Mario's.

EG: To me that comic looked very Mexican, very similar to Rius's *Los supermachos*.

GH: It was something Mario wanted to do for a long time for an American audience.

EG: I thought it was fascinating, because it had an indigenous protagonist but went about it in a completely different way to how Mexicans would portray the same story.

GH: That was his plan but, unfortunately, the story shrunk from twenty pages to six because we needed more pages for our stories. The problem with *Love and Rockets* is that we don't know how people respond to the stories. We don't. A lot of times, we change things, and we don't hear a word about it other than "we really like your comics." I don't know what happens to those stories with more obscure topics that are not linked to the *Palomar* or *Locas* sagas. You never know what they would be interested in. You saw people earlier [at the lunch] saying that they were teaching "The Ghoul Man" [a more obscure work].

JH: I was so surprised. I thought "You are teaching 'The Ghoul Man'!"

GH: But it takes readers outside of the comic book industry to appreciate these stories, and that is what I mean when I complain about the superhero ghetto.

On Gender/Queer Issues and Controversies

EG: I wanted to ask you about the portrayal of sexuality in your comics. When I teach your books, my students at Middlebury College tend to be between eighteen and twenty-one years old and are still developing their ideas about sexuality, so suddenly they are shocked when I engage them with *Poison River*. [Gilbert laughs] One of the most interesting aspects in your works is how you portray queer characters, always a controversial subject in the United States. You had previously told me that you yourselves are not gay but your work abounds in characters that embody queerness. Why do you constantly focus on these characters? Is it because they defy the conservative ideas of a homogenous heterosexual society? I learn from your characters to see the world from a different perspective, which I find the best lesson anyone can get from a narrative. Is this your intention?

GH: I think I have a chip on my shoulder. I don't like conservative thinking (don't mean Republican), I mean people who are always saying, "Don't do that." Always scaring people, that really bothers me, especially when gay people are ostracized. How dare a group of people tell other people how to behave! It's something I had in my own life. We had to keep things quiet when we were growing up because of who we were. Everyone has that going on when they grow up, but some worse than others. We just feel that with our art we express ourselves every day, every time that we get a piece of paper and we draw. In this comic book page, we feel we have a way of expressing ourselves freely, and when we hear about oppression and gay subjects, we get mad and think: How dare you bully a kid to death just because he makes you uncomfortable! I can't do anything about slavery in the past or about the Native American genocide, but I can comment on this that is going on now.

EG: One of the saddest moments in *Julio's Day* is when the main character cannot acknowledge his sexual orientation toward the end of his life, even though one of his younger relatives had already come out of the closet.

GH: I wanted to show how he was completely repressed. . . .

EG: I had family members like that who practically will take these secrets to their graves. And at some point one begins to think if one has been part of this oppression. It is interesting that you previously pointed out that being conservative is not being Republican. People raised in traditional Hispanic families, Republican and Democrat alike, often hold conservative views that have affected many gay Latinos who have been ostracized by their own communities.

GH: I don't know if I can speak for other Latino cultures, but our Mexican heritage with its machismo can be annoying sometimes. It's contradictory because the women run the houses, but the rules are set by the men. We didn't experience it too much because our father died when we were children, so we saw the feminine side of the family constantly. The hardworking feminine side, not the girly side. Naturally, when I went into the world as a young man, I loved the girly side, you could never be too feminine for me. You learn with experience that you can be feminine *and* smart, as many academic women are. But I guess that, because we had a tomboy for a mom, we were attracted to the girly types.

EG: You portray all types of women in your comics, girly, smart, etc. However, many readers in academia still take issue with your representation of women. The first time I read *Poison River*, I was in a graduate class, and I was in charge of the discussion of your book. I was all excited about the topic and praising your work, but I was shocked to realize that half of the class was offended.

GH Really, they were offended?

EG: Yes. For example, there was a female graduate student from Spain who said that she was returning the book immediately because she did not want any of her money going to the publisher. She was offended by the violent sex depicted in *Poison River*. I mean, no matter how great I think your work is, it is very difficult to know how any specific reader would react to the depiction of sex in your works. It is a lottery with my classes, too.

GH: You never know what they are going to be offended by with representations of sex.

JH: One time I did a talk with another teacher at a school because they were discussing my stuff from *Love and Rockets*, and he said that one of the students opened the book in the scene where Maggie kisses the frog's mouth, and she pushes it and says "faggot." The person saw her saying "faggot" and just slammed the book on the table. The teacher asked the person, "Did you read it?," but that was it for that reader.

EG: I thought the problem with *Poison River* in that particular discussion in my graduate class was that many associate prudishness with being conservative, but you can be a progressive liberal and also have issues with graphic sexuality. The climax of *Poison River*, when everyone achieves happiness by having sex constantly, can be controversial because even enlightened individuals could be resistant to the idea of sex equating pure happiness. I find your works more surreal in the traditional sense (like the works of Spanish director Luis Buñuel) because you project sexuality as a key to happiness that surpasses opposing ideologies. I think most people find sex very threatening.

GH: It's very threatening because it's so personal. Sometimes the complaints from the [female] readers are based on their own insecurities. They see sex from a more intellectual perspective, but don't want to be reminded that they don't like their own body. This bubble burst for me when Madonna was doing all the bondage stuff that men usually did. But because she was in charge and making the money, it was all right even though men were still getting sexually aroused. Suddenly Madonna changed the perception of female sexuality. Look at Katy Perry and others, they are out there but they are accepted because they are in control.

EG: To be fair to the casual reader, there was an issue that I found very funny in terms of visualizing sex, in which Fritz and Pipo [from *Love and Rockets*] go on a rampage and have sex with a strange guy that has two penises. I first read it in the serial comic version, and it made sense to me because I have read the entire series and I have a grasp of the story arc and how this bit fits into it. However, I think if a casual reader would glance at it he/she could be horrified because there is barely any plot in it, mostly pure sex. They would think it's porn.

GH and JH: [smile] Yeah, Yeah.

JH: I remember that. [smiles]

EG: When I read *Poison River* for the first time, it felt like a Mexican musical from the '50s, such as Ninón Sevilla's *Aventurera*. One of the interesting elements of the Mexican movies is that *mestizaje* would be represented by Cuban superstars such as Rita Montaner and Ninón Sevilla because they supposedly have "African roots." In *Poison River*, Luba's *mestizaje* is the product of the interracial affair of a rich white woman and a peasant indigenous man, something you are unlikely to see in classic Mexican cinema unless it was inverted (a rich white man having an affair with a poor indigenous woman).

GH: I did cheat with that, because why would María [Luba's mother] be with this poor guy? It doesn't make sense. I guess I didn't think it through, and because I was accustomed to have my ugly guys meet pretty girls.

JH: I guess you created him to look Indian because he needed to look like Luba [Note: *Poison River* is a prequel to Luba's *Palomar* stories].

GH: The story does not make sense. María should not have fallen for him.

EG: Maybe it does not make sense, but it breaks from the gender/race/class paradigm of traditional Mexican visual narratives.

GH: I guess that is true.

JH: I guess she could have been attracted to his differentness.

GH: Yes, but María is not that deep.

JH: Well, it's the classic story of my friend [name omitted]. Once he was talking about how he got a white girlfriend and she went to his house and they had sex, etc. He told me she was white, and I assumed she was a trashy white girl, but when I finally saw her in his yearbook, she was a cute all-American girl. My friend was dark and indigenous-looking, and I found cool that the girl had everything in the white world but was attracted to this guy. So I felt it was something like that with María.

GH: Yes, but Luba's father didn't have anything going for him. Which is why later I redraw him in a later story to be more handsome. I changed the drawing. Because why would she throw away her life with a millionaire?

JH: She didn't, she was thrown out by the husband.

GH: Right, when he found out she slept with the peasant.

JH: I still think it works. . . .

GH: Yes . . . it works. Weirder things have happened in the world.

On Latino Issues and the Politics of Immigration

EG: I wanted to ask about the differences between the *Palomar* and the *Locas* sagas. Gilbert's *Palomar* begins in a fictional Latin America and Jaime's *Locas* storylines take place mostly in the United States. When scholars write about Latino storytelling, they establish a difference between immigrant and native Latino authors. I feel that Gilbert's story resembles more the immigrant storytelling because his characters move from one (fictional) nation-state to the United States and struggle more with assimilation and their own otherness, whereas Jaime's stories have Latino characters that are native and more comfortable with their American identity in their interactions with other Americans from different backgrounds. If they would ask me what the main difference between your stories is, it is the bigger role of the Latin American space (even though it is a fictional one) in Gilbert's plot.

GH: This is the funny part about how academics perceive our work, because they talk like if we are portraying political issues, but they are not for me. For example, I just needed to move the characters to the U.S. so that I could have a new background for the characters. I could have researched the whole immigration thing, but my lazy way was to make people so rich that they could easily move here. So I cut through all of the traditional stories about the problems of immigration. There is a story there but it is not my story.

EG: But there are some characters from *Palomar* that live in the U.S., and their main problem is adjusting to the lifestyle in the U.S., right?

GH: It's like that thing we were talking earlier about people always feeling that the stories in *Love and Rockets* are sad. They also ask me: Why do the people of *Palomar* go to live in the United States? I think people grow up and move, and have different experiences. . . .

EG: Don't you think the *Palomar* characters became stronger in the United States? In the original storylines, they were at the mercy of a gringo photographer, and in the current storylines they have acquired so much wealth in the U.S. that they are creating their own B movies and therefore have the ability to tell their own story.

GH: I guess they are successful immigrants. . . .

EG: Yes, but they are involved in the process of filmmaking. Doralis writes the screenplay, Pipo provides the budget, and Fritz stars in the film. I mean, the fact that your next graphic novel is their film adaptation of *Poison River* shows how the characters have taken control of the narrative. It's a big difference from being the subjects of the American photographer at the beginning of the story.

GH: I guess that's true. I think I was straitjacketed by the original *Palomar* setting. I don't think I felt creative; it worked for me for a little while. I am interested in culture, in the things that are happening now. In this setting, the characters didn't care about anything, just their families. So I had to move them from there, because they needed to be more modern, interact with something. I don't know.

On Becoming Part of the Literary and Comic Books Canon

EG: Jaime, in the earlier lunch we had with professors and students from Ohio State, you mentioned that you were always embarrassed to talk in academic settings because you were a bad student when you were growing up. Maybe the reason your work feels so original is because you are not constricted by an academic canon with its aesthetic ideals. I mean, look at me trying to link Penny Century to Cervantes's *Don Quixote*. Still, sometimes there are creators such as Quentin Tarantino that don't have a formal education but have seen a lot of films and are able to express themselves in innovative ways. I see both of you as creators that continue to surprise me even if I had read thousands of comics as part of my specialty.

JH: Part of it is that we don't know how to sell out. We don't know how to buy into the structure. I think if I knew where I was going, I would be bored.

GH: You need the challenge, the mystery of where we are going to.

JH: If I learned to do things in a structured way, how to be successful, etc., I would be very bored. I think our comics are traditional and our drawing style has existed since the '30s. It's just that the subject matter may make it more challenging. People always ask me, "Why didn't you pick up that style?" And I say that since high school I became satisfied with the way I drew. Of course, it needed tweaking. I became satisfied when I found out that no matter what I wanted to draw, I could do it in that style. I have been drawing like that since then, except the four years I spent learning better anatomy, layouts or whatever. I stopped copying other artists by then. It was the inking that came later, when we started to learn how to ink ourselves. That style I developed allowed me to do everything from punk rockers to spaceships, and stuff like that. I don't think that was the question you asked. Sorry.

EG: One last question, how do you feel about entering the literary canon? Is this okay with you? Is it problematic?

GH: It is always a positive thing. Because [academics] discuss our works and find them interesting and talk about them, while in the comic book world, because we are not *Batman* and *Superman*, we are shoved away because we are in the way.

EG: Both of you are here in Ohio State to be the keynote speakers at the Grand Opening Festival of Cartoon Art.

JH: When people ask me to do something like this, I get nervous at first because I was a terrible student and I am coming back to school, and I feel you have to be at an academic level, and then I slap myself in the face and say, They wanted me! That happened also when the *New York Times* asked me to do the Maggie strip.

EG: What I love about your books is that I think we will be teaching them for over thirty years, but sometimes many of the Marvel and DC superhero stories become outdated and unreadable in a couple of years even if they get all the hype at the comic book conventions.

GH: True.

EG: The consequence of becoming part of the academic canon is that you will become a model for other artists to follow. . . .

GH: That is good, but I get a little nervous about that. Well, not anymore. I mean a lot of my work in *Love and Rockets* was dealing in several levels of sleaze because I grew up enjoying exploitation art. So I still get surprised sometimes, like when I was in Beverly Hills talking to an audience with Governor Jerry Brown, Harrison Ford, Kathryn Bigelow, and they are all smiling while talking about my body of work and I am like, OK, I will take it. I guess I have arrived, like Crumb. He is my model because he has done the sleaziest comics you could think of, and he is considered a national treasure. We have things in our comics that have kept us legitimate for the current audiences.

EG: I think many artists can imitate certain techniques, but I think it will be impossible to replicate what you did in *Love and Rockets*. Thirty years of continuous publishing and character development? I don't think so.

GH: That's good. [both smile]

EG: Thanks for granting me the interview.

GH and JH: You are welcome.

notes

Preface

1. Gilbert Hernandez, "Poison River," *Beyond Palomar*, 45–48.
2. One of the graduate students from Spain did not want to acknowledge any redeeming qualities about the graphic novel, and she was so offended because of the pornographic nature of the story that she said, "Odié este libro de tal manera que tan pronto lo terminé, lo devolví antes de que la tienda no me repusiera el dinero." ["I hated this book so much that I returned it before the bookstore wouldn't give me my money back."] She believed that comics should be wholesome, something I found strange, as at the time Spain had more pornographic comics much more easily available than anything on the United States market. However, this made me realize that my mistake was to assume that everyone would experience Los Bros Hernandez's books in the same way I did, even if they had different notions about how the comic book medium should work.
3. Gilbert Hernandez, "Venus Tells It Like It Is," *Luba and Her Family*, 222.
4. Hernandez, "Venus Tells It Like It Is," 222.

Introduction

1. Pérez and Quesada have introduced Latino characters and concepts in some of their superhero narratives. Nevertheless, their comics are not perceived as "ethnic" narratives.
2. Frederick Luis Aldama, *Your Brain on Latino Comics: From Gus Arriola to Los Bros Hernandez*, 35–37; 72–73; 145–47.
3. Aldama, *Your Brain on Latino Comics*, 111–18; 152–65.

4. Aldama, *Your Brain on Latino Comics*, 105.

5. In a web interview with Greg Barrios, Junot Díaz acknowledges the Los Bros impact on his work:

Q. The influence of comic book *chingones* Los Brothers Hernandez—Jaime and Beto—is very evident in *Oscar*.

A. You could say they were the secret fathers of this book. What I wanted to do was honor these Chicano brothers who had a large role in teaching me how to write.

6. Alan Moore writes, "Jaime's art balances big white and black spaces to create a world of nuance in between, just as his writing balances our big human feelings and our small human trivias to generate its incredible emotional power. Quite simply, this is one of the twentieth century's most significant comics creators at the peak of his form, with every line a wedding of classicism and cool." See more at http://www.fantagraphics.com /love-and-rockets-book-24-the-education-of-hopey-glass/.

7. Scholar Bart Beaty writes, "The most vocal participants in the wartime debate about comic books included American librarians and public school teachers. This is not surprising given the fact that the former viewed themselves as charged with protecting the nation's literary heritage and the latter saw themselves at least partially responsible for the safeguarding of American children" (*Fredric Wertham and the Critique of Mass Culture*, 106).

8. This type of debate about the benefits and political disadvantages of industrialized art had emerged in industrialist cultures, and some of the most important examples of early twentieth-century Marxist critique, such as Walter Benjamin's *The Work of Art in the Age of Mechanical Reproduction* and Theodor Adorno and Mark Honkheimer's *Dialectic of Enlightenment*, criticized the shallow politics of twentieth-century entertainment and how they were used to maintain the bourgeoisie in power.

9. Wertham further tied the problem of the comic book format into his central argument when he announced the "relatively high correlation between delinquency and reading disorders; that is to say, a disproportionate number of poor or non-readers become delinquent, and a disproportionate number of delinquents have pronounced reading disorders." Wertham condemned the comics' effect on literacy by reproducing the arguments of many early critics in the education and library field about the form (Beaty, *Fredric Wertham and the Critique of Mass Culture*, 141).

10. Beaty, *Fredric Wertham*, 149.

11. Nyberg writes, "The code was literally thrown together almost overnight, with little thought about the long term impact such a document would have. A more thoughtful less hurried approach might have resulted in a more visionary structure for the code based on the idea there should be different categories depending on the intended audience. Such a code would have paved the way for the comic book industry to cater to its child audience while at the same time considering ways it could expand its market to encompass older adolescents and young adults to help stem the loss of its audience to television" (*Seal of Approval: The History of the Comics Code*, 157).

12. Nyberg, *Seal of Approval*, 117.

13. The fall of EC comics and the harsh distribution climate after the installation of the Comics Code is explained in detail in Nyberg's *Seal of Approval: The History of the Comics Code*.

14. Under the General Standards section: "1. Crimes should never be presented in such a way as to promote distrust of the forces of law and justice, or to inspire others with a desire to imitate criminals" (Nyberg, *Seal of Approval*, 171).

15. Under the General Standards section, Part B: "1. No comic magazine shall use the word horror or terror in its title." The code also targets mass culture: "Scenes dealing with, or instruments associated with walking dead or torture shall not be used. Vampires, ghouls, and werewolves should be permitted to be used when handled in the tradition such as *Frankenstein*, *Dracula* and other high caliber literary works written by Edgar Allan Poe, Saki (H. H. Munro), Conan Doyle, and other respected authors whose works are read in schools throughout the world." The Code also contains an entire section about the depiction of marriage and sex (Nyberg, *Seal of Approval*, 172–74).

16. Nyberg, *Seal of Approval*, 158.

17. Nyberg, *Seal of Approval*, 159.

18. According to Rubenstein, "The (Mexican) publishing industry did not respond directly to its critics because there was no need to do so. The same publishers produced comic books and Mexico City newspapers, and these newspapers were important government supporters; sometimes, too, newspapers acted as mouthpieces for individual politicians, none of whom were at all likely to risk offending politicians by shutting down their profitable businesses. Publishers could use their personal connections to high level government officials to oppose the censorship campaign" (*Bad Language, Naked Ladies, and Other Threats to the Nation*, 112).

19. Anne Rubenstein, *Bad Language, Naked Ladies, and Other Threats to the Nation*, 95.

20. In Rubenstein's words: "According to Lewis, however, these new values had destroyed the prospects of the family's second generation, for while the hardworking patriarch had 'managed to raise himself out of the depths of poverty,' his children had sunk back into it. These new values were carried by the mass media, and comic books—alongside radio and cinema—were prominent in Lewis' account. He cites the fond memory of Sanchez' shiftless son Roberto, that 'my father had always brought copies of the comic magazines for Elena "the stepmother" and for us kids,' thus unwittingly setting them up for corruption." Rubenstein, "The Uses of Failure: La Comisión Calificadora," *Bad Language, Naked Ladies, and Other Threats to the Nation*, 109–32.

21. Gilbert Hernandez, "Poison River," *Beyond Palomar*, 37.

22. Todd Hignite, *The Art of Jaime Hernandez: The Secrets of Life and Death*, 37.

23. Hignite, *The Art of Jaime Hernandez*, 38.

24. Hignite writes, "Childhood interests were dominated by American popular culture, and Aurora Hernandez encouraged her kids' comics reading and collecting. She'd been an avid fan in her youth and, though she had thrown out her collection years before, her enthusiasm remained. She also drew portraits of her favorite Golden Age comic characters, from Superman to the more obscure Doll Man, Captain Triumph, and the Black Terror, which in their strange iconic power had a huge impact on Hernandez's love of the medium" (*The Art of Jaime Hernandez*, 47).

25. "Comix" is the term used by the underground artists to distinguish their work from mainstream comics.

26. Roger Sabin, *Comics, Comix and Graphic Novels: A History of Comic Art*, 94.

27. Sabin, *Comics, Comix and Graphic Novels: A History of Comic Art*, 94.

28. As Sabin explains, "Finally, in terms of marketing, the comix were ideally placed to take advantage of the existing network of hippie shops, or headshops, which were a feature of big towns in the USA and Canada. These sold trendy clothing and jewelry, plus drug paraphernalia such as pipes and reefers, as well as a selection of psychedelic posters, which were a major influence on the look of the comix. The content of the comix meant they could not possibly be sold via the traditional newsagent route, so this was a perfect alternative" (*Comics, Comix and Graphic Novels*, 94).

29. Hatfield writes, "Alternative comics trace their origins to the underground 'comix' movement of the 1960s and 1970s, which, jolted to life by the larger social upheavals of the era, departed from the familiar, anodyne conventions of the commercial comics mainstream . . ." (*Alternative Comics: An Emerging Literature*, Kindle locations 23–24).

30. Hatfield, *Alternative Comics*, Kindle locations 418–21.

31. Hatfield, *Alternative Comics*, Kindle locations 424–27.

32. Hatfield explains the role the direct market played in the creation of alternative comics: "Many of the alternative comics studied herein were born of the direct market during its 1980s heyday, when rising retail sales encouraged creative growth and, to a degree, diversification. While comic books in this period continued to be driven mainly by established genres such as the superhero (indeed superhero publishers sought to strengthen their grip on the market), the burgeoning alternative scene, rooted in the underground, urged the development of comic books that either sidestepped genre formulas or twisted them in novel ways" (*Alternative Comics*, Kindle locations 614–19).

33. Hatfield, *Alternative Comics*, Kindle locations, 558–60.

34. Matthew Pustz, *Comic Book Culture: Fanboys and True Believers*, 12.

35. Pustz, *Comic Book Culture*, 13.

36. Gilbert Hernandez, "Letter from Venus," *Luba and Her Family*, 23.

37. Hernandez, "Letter from Venus," 24.

38. Hernandez, "Letter from Venus," 37.

39. Venus's mother practices bodybuilding and thus has a fetish for superhero muscles. Hernandez, "Letter from Venus: Life on Mars," *Luba and Her Family*, 38.

40. Hernandez, "Letter from Venus: Who Cares About Love?" *Luba and Her Family*, 76.

41. Hatfield, *Alternative Comics*, Kindle locations 1312–19.

42. Hatfield, *Alternative Comics*, Kindle locations 1312–19.

43. Sometimes readers who do not know how the industry functions do not realize how hard it is to self-publish, because printing companies do not print what was ordered by customers but rather have a set minimum in order to fulfill the order. For example, if this minimum is 600 copies and only 300 copies were ordered by comic stores nationwide, this means that the creator has to pay out of pocket for the other 300 in order for the comic to be printed. The plight of the independent creator and the direct market is well explained in Tom Beland's *True Story Swear to God*, in which he experiences this dilemma and his wife finally convinces him to self-publish by saying they will give the excess comics away.

44. Aldama, *Your Brain on Latino Comics*, 184.

45. Groth, "Gary Groth and the Brothers," 32.

46. In an interview with scholar Derek Parker Royal, Gilbert explains:

We changed the format from the magazine to comic book size. This was one of the complaints about why the original *Love and Rockets* magazine didn't sell as well as it could: it didn't fit into the readers' comic boxes. Yeah, you've got to consider things like that in the market. It's ridiculous, but you do. Some readers won't buy comic books because they won't fit in their boxes. So we just went down to comic book size, and so many readers were happy. "Great, now I can fit it in with my *Superman* and *Batman* comics." That's okay/Just keep buying! ("The Worlds of the Hernandez Brothers," 236)

47. In his interview with scholar Derek Parker Royal, Gilbert discusses why they had to go back to the title *Love and Rockets*:

One of the reasons—and I'm going to sound like a cynical old fart here—was that it was difficult for readers to find our new work. We had the *Love and Rockets* umbrella title, and it worked so well for us that all the reader had to do was go into the comic store and ask, "Where is the new *Love and Rockets*?" And that was it. That's where they found our work. Then we got itchy and wanted to do our own comics with different titles, just because it was time. We wanted to stretch our elbows out a little bit. And we did our own comics [*Luba, Penny Century,* and *New Love*], but for some reason it just didn't get the same response *Love and Rockets* did. The work was the same—it was still us, with a lot of the same characters we had been using—but people just could not find our comics. . . . (Parker Royal, "The Worlds of the Hernandez Brothers," 236)

48. Parker Royal, "The Worlds of the Hernandez Brothers," n.p.
49. *Poison River* is a prequel to the *Palomar* saga, but it does not take place in Palomar. This is why it is usually not included in the *Palomar* collections.
50. Parker Royal, "Palomar and Beyond: An Interview with Gilbert Hernandez," 233.
51. Aldama, *Your Brain on Latino Comics*, 174.
52. In an interview conducted by Tim Hodler, Dan Nadel, and Frank Santoro for *The Comics Journal*, Gilbert describes how the editing policies at DC Comics forced him to provide the obscure ending for *Sloth*:

Yeah, when I don't have money, like zero in the bank, I'm working like crazy. But anyway, like I said, it was a learning experience. I had never done anything like that in one fell swoop. It was always a series or whatever. And I like the way it turned out in the end, even though it's not perfect. It's shy 4 pages, because they just wanted to get it out and I was taking way too long. There were four exposition pages that kind of explained things a little bit more. [Laughter.] Oh, we'll just blame it on David Lynch–type obscure story-telling if the story's confusing. And I give my editor credit for that. She put up with a lot. They put up with a lot. And it turned out well. It wasn't 100% mine, but I could see the problems they were having with it, because I didn't know—I was learning. (n.p.)

53. Parker Royal, "The Worlds of the Hernandez Brothers," n.p.

Chapter One. Subverting the Intertextual Comic Book Corporate Structure

1. Graham Allen writes about the transition from the structuralist to the poststructuralist period: "This transition is often characterized as one in which assertions of objectivity, scientific rigour, methodological stability and other highly rationalistic sounding terms are replaced by an emphasis on uncertainty, indeterminacy, incommunicability, subjectivity, desire, pleasure, and play" (Allen, *Intertextuality,* 3).

2. Allen, *Intertextuality*, 15.

3. Frank D'Angelo, "The Rhetoric of Intertextuality," *Rhetoric Review*, 34–35; 38.

4. Hutcheon, "Historiographic Metafiction: Parody and the Intertextuality of History," *Intertextuality and Contemporary American Fiction*, 3.

5. Roland Barthes, "The Death of the Author," *The Norton Anthology Theory and Criticism*, 1468.

6. Michel Foucault, "What Is an Author?," *The Norton Anthology Theory and Criticism*, 1628–29.

7. When discussing Balzac's role as an author, Barthes writes:

Who is speaking thus? Is it the hero of the story bent on remaining ignorant of the castrato hidden beneath the woman? Is it Balzac the individual, furnished by his personal experience with a philosophy of Woman? Is it Balzac the author professing "literary" ideas on femininity? Is it universal wisdom? Romantic psychology? we shall never know, for the good reason that writing is the destruction of every voice, of every point of origin. Writing is that neutral, composite, oblique space where our subject slips away, the negative where all identity is lost, starting with the very identity of the body writing. (Barthes, "The Death of the Author," 1466)

8. Scholar E. D. Hirsch argues in his article "In Defense of the Author" that the "death" of the author gave the power of meaning to the critics but that we still need the author to decode meaning. He writes:

Thus when critics deliberately vanished the original author, they themselves usurped his place, and this led unerringly to some of our present day theoretical confusions. Where before there had been but one author, there now arose a multiplicity of them, each carrying as much authority as the next. To banish the original author as the determiner of meaning was to reject the only compelling normative principle that could lend validity to an interpretation. On the other hand, it might be the case that there does not really exist a viable normative idea that governs the interpretations of texts. This would follow if any of the arguments brought against the author would hold. For if the meaning of the text is not the author's, then no interpretation can possibly correspond to the meaning of the text, since the text can have no determinate or determinable meaning. (Hirsch, "In Defense of the Author," *Intention and Interpretation*, 14)

9. Nancy Miller, *Subject to Change: Reading Feminist Writing*, 104.

10. Gilbert Hernandez, *Luba and Her Family*, 91–92.

11. Hernandez, *Luba and Her Family*, 92.

12. Foucault writes:

In a mathematical treatise, the ego who indicates the circumstances of composition in the preface is not identical, either in terms of his position or his function, to the "I" who concludes a demonstration within the body of the text. The former implies a unique individual who, at a given time or place, succeeded in completing a project, whereas the latter indicates an instance and plan of demonstration that anyone could perform provided the same set of axioms, preliminary operations, and an identical set of symbols were used. It is also possible to locate a third ego: one who speaks of the goal of his investigations, the obstacles encountered, its results, and the problems yet to be solved and this "I" would function in a field of future mathematical discourses. We are not dealing with a system of dependencies where a first and essential use of the "I" is reduplicated, as a kind of fiction, by the other two. On the contrary, the "author-function" in such discourses operates so as to effect the simultaneous dispersion of the three egos. (Foucault, "What Is an Author?," 1631)

13. Scott McCloud, *Understanding Comics: The Invisible Art*, 27–59.

14. McCloud, *Understanding Comics*, 60–139.

15. Hatfield, *Alternative Comics: An Emerging Literature*, Kindle locations 126–28.

16. For example, if a prose writer writes "she was drinking coffee," the authorial voice is not as explicit as seeing a drawing of Gilbert's Luba drinking coffee. A drawing will be immediately recognizable as a drawing by Gilbert, regardless of what the character is doing or how.

17. Even though the editorial board of *The Comics Journal* is often perceived in the comic book world as promoting a snobbish attitude against mainstream comics and being biased toward alternative comics, they have been receptive to certain creators that published their comics within mainstream venues but that still display an "auteur" style distinguishing them from the "sameness" of corporate mass culture. Matthew Pustz explains:

> For many years, the periodical continued to focus on contemporary mainstream comics as well as comics from the golden and silver ages. Even into the mid-1980s, the *Comics Journal* featured detailed news and reviews of mainstream superhero comics. Shortly thereafter though, the magazine's promise to cater to discerning fans meant an increasing focus on independent black-and-white comics, the emerging alternative-comics scene. By the 1990s, the *Journal* had become a magazine almost snobbishly devoted to alternative comics. Its article "The Best Comic Books Shops in America," for example, clearly emphasized selection of alternative, small press, and minicomics over (mainstream) back issue collections. The alternativity of the *Comics Journal* is now taken for granted, but occasional interviews with artists such as Joe Kubert, Gil Kane, Carmen Infantino, and Barry Windor-Smith continue to reveal Groth's roots in older, mainstream fanzines. (Pustz, *Comic Book Culture: Fanboys and True Believers*, 181)

18. Todd Hignite writes, "*Mad Magazine* was also a big deal, with Mario buying every issue off the stands as it came out. Its topical nature was as important to Hernandez as the acclaimed irreverent humor: 'That's how I knew who Kennedy was'" (Hignite, *The Art of Jaime Hernandez: The Secrets of Life and Death*, 52).

19. Gary Groth, "Gary Groth and the Brothers," *The Love and Rockets Companion*, 71.

20. In response to how Robert Crumb is criticized for his depiction of women, Gilbert Hernandez says the following in his interview with Marc Sobel:

> A few people I've known over the years say: "Aw, women are going after Crumb because they don't have a sense of humor; blah, blah." But I'll say, "You know what, if Crumb were saying that about you over and over, you'd feel pretty uncomfortable about it, too." Crumb's being honest and venting his demons, but sometimes it's hard to defend. I can't argue with a woman who gets offended because of how Crumb depicted women in a certain story. I can't say, "Oh well, you're dumb. You should learn to take a joke," because it is insulting. Jaime and I are Latino, and we've heard that kind of shit about us. We don't

like it either: So why would women like that stuff? I will say, Crumb the artist can still engage me despite the negative stuff. Maybe Crumb's just being a satirist, but it's hard to say. (Sobel, "Marc Sobel and The Brothers," *The Love and Rockets Companion*, 139)

21. Gary Groth, "One of My Main Reasons to Go On Living Is I Still Think I Haven't Done My Best Work," *R. Crumb: Interviews, Comix, and Color Gallery*, 55–56.
22. Linda Hutcheon writes:

In short, adaptation can be described as the following:

- An acknowledged transposition of a recognizable other work or works;
- A creative and an interpretive act of appropriation/salvaging;
- An extended intertextual engagement with the adapted work.

Therefore, an adaptation is a derivation that is not derivative—a work that is second without being secondary. It is its own palimpsestic thing. (*A Theory of Adaptation*, 8–9)

23. Julie Sanders, *Adaptation and Appropriation*, 26.
24. See specifically Greg Potter's analysis of Kurtzman's war story "Big If."
25. Similarly, I am unsure readers in thirty years would understand jabs at Justin Bieber or specific contestants on reality TV shows.
26. Linda Hutcheon, *A Theory of Parody*, 101.
27. Robert Petersen, *Comics, Manga, and Graphic Novels: A History of Graphic Narratives*, 206.
28. Hutcheon, *A Theory of Parody*, 38–39.
29. Hutcheon, *A Theory of Parody*, 32.
30. Harvey Kurtzman and Wally Wood, "Superduperman," *Mad Archives*, 118.
31. Jeff Jensen, "*Watchmen* and Oral History," *Entertainment Weekly* website.
32. Hutcheon, *A Theory of Parody*, 5.
33. Petersen, *Comics, Manga, and Graphic Novels*, 207.
34. Quoted in Petersen, *Comics, Manga, and Graphic Novels*, 207
35. John Benson, "Notes," *The Sincerest Form of Parody*, 33.
36. Roger Sabin, *Comics, Comix and Graphic Novels: A History of Comic Art*, 92.
37. Sabin, *Comics, Comix and Graphic Novels*, 94.
38. Hatfield, *Alternative Comics*, Kindle locations 379–81.
39. Pustz, *Comic Book Culture*, 63.
40. Hignite, *The Art of Jaime Hernandez*, 48–49; 51.
41. Bakhtin writes in his chapter "The Prehistory of the Novelistic Discourse":

The novel comes into contact with the spontaneity of the conclusive present; this is what keeps the genre from congealing. The novelist is drawn toward everything that is not yet completed. He may turn up on the field of representation in any authorial pose, he may depict real moments in his own life or make allusions to them, he may interfere in the conversation of his heroes, he may openly polemicize with his literary enemies and so forth. This is not merely a matter of the author's image appearing within his own field of representation—important here is the fact that the underlying, original formal author (the author of the authorial image) appears in a new relationship with the represented world. Both find themselves now subject to the same valorized measurements, for the "depicting" authorial language now lies on the same plane as the "depicted" language of the hero, and may enter into dialogic relations and hybrid combinations with it (indeed it cannot help but enter into such relations). (Mikhail Bakhtin, *Problems of Dostoevsky's Poetics*, 27)

42. Bakhtin, *Problems of Dostoevsky's Poetics*, 64.
43. Bakhtin, *Problems of Dostoevsky's Poetics*, 127.
44. D'Angelo, "The Rhetoric of Intertextuality," 41.
45. Fredric Jameson, *Postmodernism, or, the Cultural Logic of Late Capitalism*, 16.
46. Hutcheon, *The Politics of Postmodernism*, 13.
47. Gilbert Hernandez, "BEM," *Amor y Cohetes*, 10.
48. Hernandez, "BEM," 11.
49. Hernandez, "BEM," 11.
50. Hernandez, "BEM," 12.
51. Hernandez, "BEM," 13.
52. Hernandez, "BEM," 15.
53. Hernandez, "BEM," 12.
54. Hernandez, "BEM," 40.
55. Hernandez, "BEM," 41–46.
56. Hernandez, "BEM," 48.
57. Jaime Hernandez, "Mechan-X," *Maggie the Mechanic*, 7.
58. Hernandez, "Mechan-X," 8.
59. Hernandez, "Mechan-X," 9.
60. Hernandez, "Mechan-X," 10.
61. Hernandez, "Mechan-X," 11.
62. Hernandez, "Mechan-X," 12–13.
63. Hernandez, "Mechan-X," 14.
64. Jaime Hernandez, "Penny Century, You're Fired!," *Maggie The Mechanic*, 23.
65. Jaime Hernandez, "Maggie vs. Maniakk," *Maggie the Mechanic*, 91–92.
66. Hernandez, "Maggie vs. Maniakk," 92.
67. Hernandez, "Maggie vs. Maniakk," 93.
68. Hernandez, "Maggie vs. Maniakk," 93–94.
69. Hernandez, "Maggie vs. Maniakk," 95–98.
70. Jaime Hernandez, "Mechanics," *Maggie the Mechanic*, 39.
71. Jaime Hernandez, "Bay of Threes," *Penny Century*, 237–49.
72. Gilbert Hernandez says that the story works for Jaime because it is based on his own characters: "Yes, that's right. Yeah, I was toying with the superhero comic idea but the bottom line is I have absolutely no idea how to write a story that's interesting, that's something worth reading. See Jaime's stuff is connected to the Maggie world. So it flowers from that. It flowers from the certain characters he's already done and you put them in that world, so it starts to build. If I go in cold like that, I don't know what to do" (Tim Hodler, Dan Nadel, and Frank Santoro, "The Gilbert and Jaime Hernandez Interview," *The Comics Journal*, web).
73. In an interview about his superhero adventure, Jaime downplays the interpretation of his work as a deconstruction of superhero myths. He says, "Yeah, I also felt that superhero fans these days are holding onto this thing to make superheroes worth reading. They have this thing about the myth of the superhero and stuff, and I think, I'm guessing that's what didn't have the soul in it, that I didn't follow the myth of the superhero, which I didn't

care about, 'cause I don't know what the hell the myth of the superhero is . . . [Laughter.]" (Hodler, Nadel, and Santoro, "The Gilbert and Jaime Hernandez Interview," web).

74. Jaime Hernandez, "Day by Day with Hopey: Friday Is Jai Alai Day," *Esperanza*, 172.

75. In an interview with Tim Hodler, Dan Nadel, and Frank Santoro, Jaime says that this superhero story was improvised: "I just didn't have a superhero story 'til now—I kept putting it in the background in the regular comics, and there was the time Gilbert said, 'I want to do a superhero comic on the side, a color comic.' He goes, 'One that doesn't make sense, like an old '40s one that has no explanation, just superhero stuff.' And I was like, 'Huh, yeah, that'd be cool'" (Hodler, Nadel, and Santoro, "The Gilbert and Jaime Hernandez Interview," web).

76. Jaime explains in an interview with Tim Hodler, Dan Nadel, and Frank Santoro that his intertextual allusions in "The Return of the Ti-Girls" were made due to his inability to come up with new designs for female characters:

> It was . . . it's a long story. [Laughter.] It goes back to that, when I started creating them, I was going, "Oh my God, I'm creating more characters that look like other characters." So that's when I came up with that twisty thing of, "Hey, why doesn't it be some old characters in a different dimension." It's "Hey, Rocky is the Weeper. I'll use Mini Rivero as Golden Girl, and then she looked a lot like Xochitl." But in the end, she didn't really. I mean, if you look at Xochitl there's similarities, but she really didn't and I thought, "Why, I guess I didn't have to after all." So that's why I kinda made it when she and Maggie meet—Maggie goes, "I've got a cousin that kinda looks like her." [Laughter.] So that just made it even more that this dimension, this different dimension thing was weird, there was more to it than just, we're the same people in this dimension, too, but we have different roles. [Laughter] I was covering my ass a lot. (Hodler, Nadel, and Santoro, "The Gilbert and Jaime Hernandez Interview," web)

77. Jaime Hernandez, *God and Science: Return of the Ti-Girls*, 8–9.

78. Hernandez, *God and Science*, 11.

79. Hernandez, *God and Science*, 16–19.

80. Hernandez, *God and Science*, 12–13.

81. Hernandez, *God and Science*, 131. This particular ending was expanded in the graphic novel version of the story and did not appear in the original resolution to the storyline that was published in the third volume of *Love and Rockets*. The original ending was more open-ended.

82. Hernandez, *God and Science*, 73.

83. As Linda Hutcheon writes, "There are many possible forms of the ethos of parody: is it intended as innocently reverential? ridiculing? didactic? mnemonic? ironic? Does it accept or resist the Other? In any case, of course, the very act of parodying invests the Other with both authority and an exchange value in relation to literary norms. These norms are like social ones in the sense that they are human constructs which are authoritative only to those who have constructed or at least accepted them as *a priori*" (Hutcheon, *A Theory of Parody*, 77).

84. Hernandez, *God and Science*, 125–26.

85. Hernandez, *God and Science*, 128.

86. Hernandez, *God and Science*, 128.

Spotlight 2. Robots in Jaime's "Rocky" Stories and Gilbert's *Citizen Rex*

1. Jaime Hernandez, "Rocky's Birthday Surprise," 166.

Chapter Two. The Revision of Latino Experience through Comic Book Genres and Soap Opera Devices in Gilbert's *Palomar* and Jaime's *Locas* Sagas

1. Derek Parker Royal confirms this: "What is more, the sexuality represented is largely fluid and nonconventional, leaving the reader to question the role of heteronormativity in the narrative. Homosexuality, bisexual encounters, fetishism, and other sexual practices are represented in such a way that all become normative within the worlds of 'Love and Rockets'" ("Hernandez Brothers' *Love and Rockets*," 523).

2. Gracia writes, "First, in order to know ourselves and our present reality, we need to go back to our history not only because we are its product, but also because our identity is fundamentally historical. Second, in order to liberate ourselves and open the doors to future change and development, we need to study the conditions that govern our present existence and put those conditions in context. We must look back in order to look forward; our past horizon is part of our future horizon insofar as they meet in an intangible and ever moving present" (Jorge J. E. Gracia, *Hispanic/Latino Identity: A Philosophical Perspective*, 88).

3. Ramon Saldívar, *Chicano Narrative: The Dialectics of Difference*, 215.

4. Felix Padilla writes, "The various meanings assigned to the idea or concept of Hispanic or Latino indicate quite clearly that it represents an apparent mechanism to pursue, in some instances, the collective interests of some Spanish-speaking groups. This will then mean that as Spanish-speaking people begin to adopt a consciousness as 'Latinos,' they appear to represent a distinctive, all-embracing interest-group population" (*Latino Ethnic Consciousness: The Case of Mexican Americans and Puerto Ricans in Chicago*, 66).

5. Marissa Lopez explains:

Nativism may have created a de facto Latina/o collectivity in the Anglo-American imagination, but many Latin American groups were resistant to such identification. Pérez Rosales maintains Chilean superiority in his narrative, and Mariano Vallejo was certainly no friends to Chileans. His animosity historically grounds twentieth-century Chicana/o resistance to terms like "Hispanic" and "Latino." That resistance is often understood as opposition to the homogenizing moves of Anglo capital, but it also grows from intra-communal tensions between differently located Latina/o collectivities whose resistance to Anglo hegemony engenders a vision of the past that idealizes the Mexican presence in the Southwest at the expense of other *latinidades*." (*Chicano Nations: The Hemispheric Origins of Mexican American Literature*, 57)

6. Gracia, *Hispanic/Latino Identity*, 89.

7. Torres-Saillant, "Epilogue: Problematic Paradigms: Racial Diversity and Corporate Identity in the Latino Community," *Latinos: Remaking America*, 441.

8. Torres-Saillant, "Epilogue," 444.

9. Torres-Saillant, "Epilogue," 447.

10. Jaime Hernandez, "Wigwam Bam," *Perla La Loca: A Love and Rockets Book*, 11.

11. Hernandez, "Wigwam Bam," 19.

12. Todd Hignite, *The Art of Jaime Hernandez: The Secrets of Life and Death*, 155.

13. Derek Parker Royal, "Palomar and Beyond: An Interview with Gilbert Hernandez," *MELUS*, 223.

14. Jennifer Glaser has written about Junot Díaz's relationship with Los Bros Hernandez:

Dominican-American novelist Junot Díaz has stated that he wrote *The Brief Wondrous Life of Oscar Wao* (2007) in order to finish the work the Hernandez brothers had started in *Love and Rockets*. In an interview with La Bloga, a blog devoted to Latino literature and the arts, he shares that "they were the secret fathers of [his] book" (Díaz). Oscar Wao was an attempt "to honor these Chicano brothers who had a large role in teaching [him] how to write" (Díaz). Throughout Díaz's landmark novel, references to the Hernandez brothers are synecdochic for the hybridity of Latino pop cultural production. Moreover, Díaz places the Hernandez brothers in a genealogy of transnational Latin American and Caribbean artists and thinkers that includes Édouard Glissant, Derek Walcott, Patric Chamoiseau, Aimé Cesaire, and others. Díaz singles out Gilbert Hernandez for praise, arguing that "for those of us who are writing across or on borders . . . he was . . . more important than anyone else. The stories he was writing on Palomar were recognizable to [those of us] who grew up in the Third World, in a way that made everything else seem shabby and familiar. And his eye is stupendous" (Díaz quoted in Timberg). Díaz says that "[i]n a real world, not the screwed-up world we have now, he would be considered one of the greatest American storytellers" (Díaz quoted in Timberg). He also admits that Belícia Cabral, Oscar's mother and the diasporic matriarch of *The Brief Wondrous Life of Oscar Wao*, was modeled on Luba, the "large-breasted woman with a challenging past" in Hernandez's comics (Jaggi). (Jennifer Glaser, "Picturing the Transnational in Palomar: Gilbert Hernandez and the Comics of the Borderlands," *ImageTexT: Interdisciplinary Comics Studies*, n.pag.)

15. Juan González, *Harvest of Empire: A History of Latinos in America*, xv.

16. Vernon Lattin, "Contemporary Chicano Novel, 1959–1979," *Chicano Literature: A Reference Guide*, 192.

17. Lattin, "Contemporary Chicano Novel," 184.

18. Lattin, "Contemporary Chicano Novel," 186. Héctor Calderón and José David Saldívar have written about this ideological motif: "From our vantage point in the 20th century, we can posit that such a perspective must have emerged in the borderlands in mid-nineteenth century when Mexican-Americans, Chicanos, or mestizos began to project for themselves a positive, but also critical, rendering of their bilingual and bicultural experience as a resistive measure against Anglo-American economic domination and ideological hegemony" (Héctor Calderón and José D. Saldívar, "Editors' Introduction: Criticism in the Borderlands," *Criticism in the Borderlands: Studies in Chicano Literature, Culture, and Ideology*, 4).

19. Calderón and Saldívar, "Editors' Introduction," 5.

20. "Perhaps Chicano literature has overvalued the Chicano experience, showing a sense of cultural piety for its origins. And perhaps Chicano ideologues have overstated their cultural cause. One thing is certain. The significance of a literary work does not lie simply in the social reality in which a writer participates, but it grows out of the culture that nourishes the writer" (Felipe Ortego y Gasca, "Chicano Literature from 1942 to the Present," *Chicano Literature: A Reference Guide*, 147).

21. Gary Groth, "Gary Groth and The Brothers," *The Love and Rockets Companion*, 74.

22. Parker Royal writes:

In other words, their ethnicity is more of a means through which they tell their tales, not necessarily the focus or the subject matter of their narratives. As a result, the various stories in *Love and Rockets* are particular while at the same time they transcend their contexts. The Hernandez brothers have shown that one can be ethnic without having to make that the grand sum of one's comics. All in all, the characters created by the Hernandez brothers are familiar to us because they grow and develop as we do and, as their stories evolve, are filled with the same kind of conflicts and contradictions that define their readers." (Derek Parker Royal, "The Worlds of the Hernandez Brothers," *ImageTexT: Interdisciplinary Comics Studies*, web)

23. Gary Groth, "Gary Groth and The Brothers," *The Love and Rockets Companion*, 74

24. Groth, "Gary Groth and The Brothers," *The Love and Rockets Companion*, 74.

25. Gilbert acknowledges that he lived in a Mexican community but within a multi-racial multinational neighborhood: "The street we lived on probably had more Mexicans because the houses were inexpensive. Just a street away the kids were black or Japanese. It was a well-mixed area" (Groth, "Gary Groth and the Brothers," 12).

26. When answering Derek Parker Royal's question about his political intent, Gilbert admits,

Yes, that's how I work best. I have looked into doing overtly political stuff, but it's just not my bag, man. It's just not my strength. I don't have a journalistic or reporter's bone in me. I feel things out more. I'll respond to certain political issues, but I don't go after them directly . . . I have put political views into character's mouths that I didn't agree with at all, but I put them into sympathetic characters so that I could give the readers some balance. I will not make black and white characters; they'll always be grey. So even if I wince when I put what I think is a bad political view into an endearing character, I'll do it, because that's the way the world is. At least, that's how I see it. (Parker Royal, "Palomar and Beyond," 230)

27. Ana Merino, "The Bros Hernandez: A Latin Presence in Alternative U.S. Comics," *Redrawing the Nation: National Identity in Latin/o American Comics*, 262.

28. Groth, "Gary Groth and The Brothers," 29.

29. Gilbert remembers, "Yeah, it made me cocky enough that I could do a comic book, and it was good and it was all-right, as opposed to being intimidated by the Marvel guys. As lousy as they were, at least they could draw buildings. I could not draw buildings unless I made them up, and that intimidated me. And so with punk, I took the musical anarchy to comics" (Groth, "Gary Groth and The Brothers," 29).

30. Michelle Habell-Pallán, *Loca Motion: The Travels of Chicana and Latina Popular Culture*, 46.

31. Mendiola directed the short *Pretty Vacant* (33 min., 16mm, 1996), about a Sex Pistols–obsessed Chicana punk rocker (Habell-Pallán, *Loca Motion*, 73).

32. Habell-Pallán, *Loca Motion*, 45.

33. Sonia Saldívar-Hull, *Feminism on the Border*: *Chicana Gender Politics and Literature*, 212.

34. Saldívar-Hull, *Feminism on the Border*, 213.

35. Gilbert says, "I got mostly positive feedback. I would get letters from Puerto Ricans, Colombians, people from Cuba, and they would ask, 'How did you know?!' But that's the trick, to help readers project a part of themselves into it, and that's why they enjoy it so much, I think" (Parker Royal, "Palomar and Beyond," 228).

36. "Once in a while I'd get someone freaking out and saying, 'Hey, this is not me. You're not doing me.' But I didn't get too much of it because I made my Palomar work reflect a more general Latino culture. It looks close to Mexico, but I really wanted any Latino from anywhere to feel like they belonged there. That's why I never located it specifically in the real world. It was sort of a parallel universe where anyone could fit. It was a little town in the desert where the desert ends with the ocean. So on the one hand I could have a tropical side to it and on the other side of the town a dry desert atmosphere. It's all mythical, and I think that readers of all Latino backgrounds could place themselves there" (Parker Royal, "Palomar and Beyond," 228).

37. Groth, "Gary Groth and The Brothers," 59.

38. Frederick Aldama, *Your Brain on Latino Comics: From Gus Arriola to Los Bros Hernandez*, 178.

39. Groth, "Gary Groth and The Brothers," 13.

40. Jennifer Glaser writes:

> If diaspora is about the maintenance of identity across space and time, the Hernandez brothers depict diasporic identities by playing with the inseparability of space and time in the comics medium. The work of the Hernandez brothers (as comics artists Gilbert, Jaime, and Mario Hernandez have come to be called) has long provided an important space for the analysis of the making of transnational identities (6). Particularly, Gilbert Hernandez's "Heartbreak Soup" stories and the dense social world of Palomar that they describe provide a productive entryway to discuss transnationalism and comics. In his detailed depiction of both Central America and the U.S., Hernandez constructs an "imaginative geography" for Chicano border and Mexican diasporic identities (Said 1978, 54). I contend not only that Gilbert Hernandez's work is transnational in character and spirit, but also that the comics medium itself is often a fundamentally transnational enterprise. (Glaser, "Picturing the Transnational in Palomar," n. pag.)

41. Aldama, *Your Brain on Latino Comics*, 175–76.

42. Darcy Sullivan, "At the Drawing Board with Gilbert," *Ten Years of Love and Rockets: 1982–1992*, 28.

43. Sullivan, "At the Drawing Board with Gilbert," 28.

44. Glaser, "Picturing the Transnational in Palomar," n. pag.

45. Groth, "Gary Groth and The Brothers," 59.

46. Bill Ashcroft, "Chicano Transnation," *Imagined Transnationalism: U.S. Latino/a Literature, Culture, and Identity*, 14.

47. Nicolás Kanellos, "Exiles, Immigrants, and Natives: Hispanic Print Culture in What Became the Mainland of the United States," *A History of the Book in America, Volume 4: Print in Motion: The Expansion of Publishing and Reading in the United States, 1880–1940*, 315.

48. One has to be careful not to generalize the immigrant experience. Many Mexicans did hope to return home, and this experience is reflected in novels such as Daniel Venegas' *The Adventures of Don Chipote* (1929), which parodied the lives of immigrants in the

U.S., and suggested that they should return to the motherland (Kanellos, "Exiles, Immigrants, and Natives," 321).

49. Kanellos, "Exiles, Immigrants, and Natives," 336.

50. Anderson explains the dangers of long-distance nationalism in the following manner:

> Nonetheless, in general, today's long-distance nationalism strikes one as a probably menacing portent for the future. First of all, it is the product of capitalism's remorseless, accelerating transformation of all human societies. Second, it creates a serious politics that is at the same time radically unaccountable. The participant rarely pays taxes in the country in which he does his politics; he is not answerable to its judicial system; he probably does not cast even an absentee ballot in its election because he is a citizen in a different place; he need not fear prison, torture, or death, nor need his immediate family. But, well and safely positioned in the First World, he can send money and guns, circulate propaganda, and build intercontinental computer information circuits, all of which can have incalculable consequences in the zones of their ultimate destinations. Third, his politics, unlike those of activists for global human rights or environmental causes, are neither intermittent nor serendipitous. They are deeply rooted in consciousness that his exile is self-chosen and that the nationalism he claims on e-mail is also the ground on which an embattled ethnic identity is to be fashioned in the ethnicized nation-state that he remains determined to inhabit. That same metropole that marginalizes and stigmatizes him simultaneously enables him to play, in a flash, on the other side of the planet, national hero. (Benedict Anderson, "Long-Distance Nationalism," *The Spectre of Comparisons: Nationalism, Southeast Asia, and the World*, 74)

51. Scholar Jolle Demmers explains the differences between the nationalist visions of the diaspora and the homeland: "Since diaspora communities are physically separated from the 'core' conflict, they are engaged in different contradictions-attitudes-behavior dynamics. Even if the diaspora and the 'homeland' communities have similar perceptions of the contradiction . . . Whereas the homeland groups that are physically engaged in the conflict will experience fear, hunger, pain, and stress, diaspora groups will probably feel anger, frustration or alienation. Consequently, these differences in attitudes will effect their behavior, a change in attitudes, and transforming the relationships or clashing interests that are at the core of the conflict structure" (Demmers, "Diaspora and Conflict: Locality, Long-Distance Nationalism, and Delocalisation of Conflict Dynamics," *Diasporic Communication*, 95).

52. Mario Hernandez, *Citizen Rex*, 6.

53. Silvia Oroz, *Melodrama: El cine de lágrimas de América latina*, 21–29.

54. Muriel Cantor and Suzanne Pingree, *The Soap Opera*, 20.

55. Cantor and Pingree, *The Soap Opera*, 23.

56. Cantor and Pingree, *The Soap Opera*, 22.

57. Cantor and Pingree, *The Soap Opera*, 25.

58. Harold Hinds Jr. and Charles Tatum, *Not Just for Children: The Mexican Comic Book in the Late 1960s and 1970s*, 59.

59. Cantor and Pingree, *The Soap Opera*, 82; 28–29.

60. Hinds and Tatum, *Not Just for Children*, 61.

61. Her deceased mother never appears on the pages of the comic, and we never find

out her racial makeup. However, it is made clear that María Isabel looks like her mother and, based on María Isabel's visual representation, one may assume that the mother was white or mestiza.

62. What is interesting to see in *María Isabel* is the clash of races set in Mexico because it mimics some of the clashes that are heavily featured in Chicano literature as María Isabel is defying the rules imposed by the hegemonic white Mexican. This discourse is similar to the "us vs. white American culture" one used by Los Bros to depict how their Latino comics fit into the Anglophone hegemony. However, this can be controversial due to the fact that scholars are still trying to define the difference between racial and ethnic otherness and how they are or are not tied together. Because sometimes Latinos/Chicanos/Puerto Ricans are perceived as racial in certain American circles, the Latino artists construct their narratives to defy racial parameters. This was pointed out by Neil Gaiman in his interview with Gilbert and Jaime, where he explained that as a European he saw them as American and white because he had different parameters for the Americans. He used himself as an example of how American media would also commodify the British characters, although in a different manner. At the end of the discussion, it is clear that the topic of the racialization of the Latino will always be controversial.

63. María Isabel takes the baby to Mexico City and, thanks to her religious piety, she survives the exploitation of the rich and the desires of unscrupulous men. She finally acquires a decent job as the maid of a widower who is an intellectual and a brilliant sculptor, and they eventually connect and get married. This social event rewards her chastity and, as a consequence, guarantees her a legal position in the Mexican upper classes. However, the plot does not end there. At some point in the story, María Isabel and her husband move to Paris, the "center of civilization."

This transnational move is also similar to the *Palomar* saga, as "civilization" is perceived as located abroad. In Paris, the protagonist encounters a new antagonist when a former lover of her husband reappears. The rival is a talented Mexican pianist and very refined woman, the ideal Eurocentric Mexican female, and suddenly the husband begins to be attracted to her. María Isabel tries to educate herself to be able to compete with her husband's possible lover but gives up because she realizes that she is at a disadvantage. However, her faith is rewarded when her rival rejects María Isabel's husband because the protagonist is a "good woman."

64. Rafael Pérez-Torres, *Mestizaje: Critical Uses of Race in Chicano Culture*, 16.

65. Glaser, "Picturing the Transnational in Palomar," n. pag.

66. Charles Hatfield, *Alternative Comics: An Emerging Literature*, Kindle locations 1405–8.

67. This argument was developed by scholar Charles Hatfield, who explains that Gilbert's ability to reconcile naturalism with caricatural abstraction is one of the peculiar characteristics of the *Palomar* saga:

At the very least, we should observe that Hernandez's style, though superficially plain, is complex insofar as it reconciles naturalism with caricatural abstraction. In fact, Hernandez employs a sliding scale of realism, drawing some characters, such as children or comical stock characters, broadly and wildly, but other characters, such as many of the prominent adults in Palomar, in a restrained, naturalistic way. Such inconsistency is native to the art of cartooning, but Hernandez goes further, at times drawing even his most naturalistic characters with cartoony abandon, especially when they are in the grip of strong feelings like fear or rage (a technique widely practiced among Japanese comic artists but less common in the U.S.). (Charles Hatfield, "Heartbreak Soup: The Interdependency of Theme and Form," *Inks: Cartoon and Comic Art Studies, 6)*

68. "Garabato" means "doodle" in Spanish, so the town's name roughly translates as "Saint Doodle."

69. David Foster, *From Mafalda to Los Supermachos: Latin American Graphic Humor as Popular Culture*, 97.

70. Gilbert Hernandez, *Human Diastrophism*, 76–77.

71. Glaser, "Picturing the Transnational in Palomar," n. pag.

72. Hatfield, *Alternative Comics*, Kindle locations 1697–99.

73. Hinds and Tatum, *Not Just for Children*, 81.

74. Gilbert Hernandez, *Heartbreak Soup*, 39.

75. Hernandez, *Heartbreak Soup*, 53.

76. Hernandez, *Heartbreak Soup*, 87; Hernandez, *Human Diastrophism*, 13.

77. Hernandez, *Heartbreak Soup*, 228–39.

78. Hernandez, *Heartbreak Soup*, 222.

79. Hernandez, *Heartbreak Soup*, 216.

80. Hatfield, *Alternative Comics*, Kindle locations 1541–42. Other scholars have discussed more broadly the role of modernist movements in political art. For example, Chela Sandoval writes, "The preceding modernist Euro-American cultural epoch was, in part, eclipsed through its own proliferation. Modernist aesthetic forms once were capable of parodying, and reproducing life. They worked by creating and inspiring resistant and oppositional responses to dominant cultural forms. But today, modernist works can no longer similarly stimulate or engage a first world sensibility" (Sandoval, *Methodology of the Oppressed*, 189).

81. Scholar Caroline Hau explores in an article the conflicting role of the intellectual in third world movements, studying figures like Mao and Fanon and the existing ambivalence toward intellectual figures even in cases in which they support the subaltern's cause. She writes, "But the valorization of intellectual praxis is also often strongly inflected by an ambivalence toward the intellectual. Understandably enough, this ambivalence is an ambivalence about the status of error in intellectualism—about epistemic failure. The ambivalence, in other words, is about the intellectual's ability to *successfully* articulate the conditions and aspirations of the people" (Hau, "On Representing Others: Intellectuals, Pedagogy, and the Uses of Error," *Reclaiming Identity: Realist Theory and the Predicament of Postmodernism*, 135).

82. Gilbert Hernandez, *Beyond Palomar*, 32.

83. Hernandez, *Beyond Palomar*, 38.

84. Hernandez, *Beyond Palomar*, 35.

85. Hernandez, *Beyond Palomar*, 36–37.

86. Hernandez, *Beyond Palomar*, 36.

87. Christopher Pizzino, "Autoclastic Icons: Bloodletting and Burning in Gilbert Hernandez's Palomar," *ImageTexT: Interdisciplinary Comics Studies*, web.

88. Hernandez, *Heartbreak Soup*, 238.

89. F. Vance Neill, "Gilbert Hernandez as a Rhetor," *ImageTexT: Interdisciplinary Comics Studies*, web.

90. Frederick Aldama, "Mood, Mystery, and Demystification in Gilbert Hernandez's Twentieth-First-Century NeoNoir Stand-Alones," *ImageTexT: Interdisciplinary Comics Studies*, n. pag.

91. Aldama, *Your Brain on Latino Comics*, 105.

92. Sandoval, *Methodology of the Oppressed*, 183.

93. Aldama, *Your Brain on Latino Comics*, 187.

94. Solvej Schou, "'Love and Rockets' Co-creator Jaime Hernandez on the Comic's 30th Anniversary," *EW.com*.

95. Habell-Pallán, *Loca Motion*, 90.

96. Esther Saxey, "Desire Without Closure in Jaime Hernandez' Love and Rockets," *ImageTexT: Interdisciplinary Comics Studies*.

97. Jaime Hernandez, "Maggie vs. Maniakk," *Maggie the Mechanic*, 98.

98. "Bay of Threes," *Penny Century*, 237–49.

99. Maggie's aunt Vicki tries to debunk Rena's revolutionary mythology in Jaime Hernandez's "House of Raging Women" (*The Girl from H.O.P.P.E.R.S.*, 29).

100. In chapter 1, I already discussed the evolution of Maggie's relationship with Penny Century. Particularly relevant to my argument were Maggie's ability to access the superhero genre before Penny and Jaime's parody of the narrative structure of the genre, which he constructed by ridiculing the plots and the pathetic overbearing masculinity of both the heroes and the villains. Maggie is not interested in continuing living in this genre, which makes Penny jealous, as she has always dreamt of having access to these fantasies. This quest is finally fulfilled in the "Return of the Ti-Girls" storyline, which was later collected in the hardcover graphic novel *God and Science: Return of the Ti-Girls*.

101. Jaime Hernandez, *Maggie the Mechanic*, 31.

102. Hernandez, *Maggie the Mechanic*, 33.

103. Hernandez, *Maggie the Mechanic*, 33.

104. Hernandez, *Maggie the Mechanic*, 45.

105. Hernandez, *Maggie the Mechanic*, 52.

106. Hernandez, "House of Raging Women," 27–30.

107. This occurs in the revised version of the storyline that he published as a hardcover, *God and Science: Return of the Ti-Girls*, 134.

108. Jaime Hernandez, "La Maggie La Loca," *New York Times*, 2006, 20–21.

109. Hernandez, "La Maggie La Loca," 30–31.

110. Raquel Olea discusses this new type of contemporary feminism in her article "Feminism: Modern or Postmodern." She writes:

> The egalitarian and rights-oriented feminism produced by modernity has given way in the last twenty years to a more all-embracing theoretical-political questioning of the structures of power. Some have called this new kind of feminism, which insists on operationalizing the concept of difference as the expression of a minority social subject always deferred by masculine power, postfeminism. I prefer the notion of a feminism of difference, which is marked by its engagement with poststructuralist thought. It problematizes critically the uses of the concept of difference, sexual difference, the difference of women's experience, and how difference as a signified fixes subject position. As such, it also takes on the debate

between pro- and antiessentialist positions as ways of understanding male-female gender difference. (*The Postmodernism Debate in Latin America*, 198)

111. Hutcheon, *The Politics of Postmodernism*, 3.

Spotlight 3. "Chiro the Indian" (from *Love and Rockets: New Stories #1*, vol. 1)

1. Mario Hernandez and Gilbert Hernandez, "Chiro the Indian," *Love and Rockets: New Stories #1*, vol.1, 62.
2. Hernandez and Hernandez, "Chiro the Indian," 63–64.
3. Hernandez and Hernandez, "Chiro the Indian," 66.

bibliography

Aldama, Frederick Luis. "Mood, Mystery, and Demystification in Gilbert Hernandez's Twentieth-First-Century NeoNoir Stand-Alones." *ImageTexT: Interdisciplinary Comics Studies* 7.1 (2013). http://www.english.ufl.edu/imagetext /archives/v7_1/aldama/.

Aldama, Frederick Luis. *Your Brain on Latino Comics: From Gus Arriola to Los Bros Hernandez.* Austin: University of Texas Press, 2009.

Allen, Graham. *Intertextuality.* New York: Routledge, 2000.

Anderson, Benedict. "Long-Distance Nationalism." In *The Spectre of Comparisons: Nationalism, Southeast Asia, and the World,* 58–76. London and New York: Verso Books, 1998.

Ashcroft, Bill. "Chicano Transnation." In *Imagined Transnationalism: U.S. Latino/a Literature, Culture, and Identity,* 13–28. New York: Palgrave Macmillan, 2009.

Bagge, Peter, and Gilbert Hernandez. *Yeah!* Seattle: Fantagraphics Books, 2011.

Bakhtin, Mikhail. *Problems of Dostoevsky's Poetics.* 7th ed. Minneapolis: University of Minnesota Press, 1984.

Barrios, Gregg. "Guest Interview: Junot Díaz" (blog), October 21, 2007. http:// labloga.blogspot.com.

155

Barthes, Roland. "The Death of the Author." In *The Norton Anthology Theory and Criticism*, 1466–70. Edited by Vincent B. Leitch. New York: W. W. Norton & Company, 2001.

Beaty, Bart. *Fredric Wertham and the Critique of Mass Culture*. Jackson: University of Mississippi Press, 2005; University of Texas Press, 2009.

Beland, Tom. *True Story Swear to God*. Vol. 1. Berkeley: Image Comics, 2008.

Benson, John. "Notes." *The Sincerest Form of Parody*, 33. Seattle: Fantagraphics Books, 2012.

Calderón, Héctor, and José D. Saldívar, eds. "Editors' Introduction: Criticism in the Borderlands." In *Criticism in the Borderlands: Studies in Chicano Literature, Culture, and Ideology*, 1–10. Durham, NC: Duke University Press, 1991.

Cantor G, Muriel, and Suzanne Pingree. *The Soap Opera*. Beverly Hills: Sage Publications, 1983.

Crumb, Robert. *The Life and Death of Fritz the Cat*. Seattle: Fantagraphics Books, 2012.

D'Angelo, Frank J. "The Rhetoric of Intertextuality." *Rhetoric Review* 29:1 (2009): 31–47.

Demmers, Jolle. "Diaspora and Conflict: Locality, Long-Distance Nationalism, and Delocalisation of Conflict Dynamics." *Diasporic Communication* 9:1 (2002): 85–96.

Díaz, Junot. *This Is How You Lose Her*. Deluxe ed. New York: Riverhead Books, 2013.

Foster, David William. *From Mafalda to Los Supermachos: Latin American Graphic Humor as Popular Culture*. Boulder, CO: Lynne Rienner Publishers, 1989.

Foucault, Michel. "What Is an Author?" In *The Norton Anthology Theory and Criticism*, 1622–36. Edited by Vincent B. Leitch. New York: W. W. Norton & Company, 2001.

Gaiman, Neil. *The Best American Comics 2010*. Boston: Houghton Mifflin Harcourt, 2010.

Gaiman, Neil. "The Hernandez Brothers." *The Comics Journal* 178 (1995): 91–123.

Gaiman, Neil. "Neil Gaiman and the Brothers." In *The Love and Rockets Companion*, 80–119. Edited by Marc Sobel and Kristy Valenti. Seattle: Fantagraphics Books, 2013.

Garcia, Enrique. "Coon Imagery in Will Eisner's *The Spirit* and Yolanda Vargas Duché's *Memín Pinguín* and Its Legacy in the Contemporary United States and Mexican Comic Book Industries." *International Journal of Comic Art* 12:2/3 (Fall 2010): 112–24.

Glaser, Jennifer. "Picturing the Transnational in Palomar: Gilbert Hernandez and the Comics of the Borderlands." *ImageTexT: Interdisciplinary Comics Studies* 7.1 (2013). http://www.english.ufl.edu/imagetext/archives/v7_1/glaser/.

González, Christopher. "Turf, Tags, and Territory: Spatiality in Jaime Hernandez's 'Vida Loca: The Death of Speedy Ortiz.'" *ImageTexT: Interdisciplinary Comics Studies* 7.1 (2013). http://www.english.ufl.edu/imagetext/archives/v7_1/gonzalez/.

Gonzalez, Juan. *Harvest of Empire: A History of Latinos in America.* New York: Viking Press, 2000.

Gracia, Jorge J. E. *Hispanic/Latino Identity: A Philosophical Perspective.* Malden, MA: Wiley-Blackwell, 1999.

Groth, Gary. "Gary Groth and the Brothers." In *The Love and Rockets Companion*, 10–79. Edited by Marc Sobel and Kristy Valenti. Seattle: Fantagraphics Books, 2013.

Groth, Gary. "One of My Main Reasons to Go On Living Is I Still Think I Haven't Done My Best Work." In *The Comics Journal Library, Vol. 3: R. Crumb: Interviews, Essays, Color Gallery and Drawings*, 13–66. Seattle: Fantagraphics Books, 2004.

Habell-Pallán, Michelle. *Loca Motion: The Travels of Chicana and Latina Popular Culture.* New York: New York University Press, 2005.

Hames-García, Michael. "Queer Theory Revisited." In *Gay Latino Studies: A Critical Reader.* Edited by Michael Hames-García. Durham, NC: Duke University Press, 2011.

Hatfield, Charles. *Alternative Comics: An Emerging Literature.* Mississippi: University Press of Mississippi, 2005. Kindle edition.

Hatfield, Charles. "Heartbreak Soup: The Interdependency of Theme and Form." *Inks: Cartoon and Comic Art Studies* 4.2 (May 1997): 2–17.

Hau, Caroline. "On Representing Others: Intellectuals, Pedagogy, and the Uses of Error." In *Reclaiming Identity: Realist Theory and the Predicament of Postmodernism*, 133–70. Edited by Paula M. L. Moya and Michael R. Hames-García. Berkeley, Los Angeles, and London: University of California Press, 2000.

Hernandez, Gilbert. "BEM." In *Amor y Cohetes*, 9–48. Seattle: Fantagraphics Books, 2008.

Hernandez, Gilbert. *Beyond Palomar.* Seattle: Fantagraphics Books, 2007.

Hernandez, Gilbert. *Bumperhead.* Montreal: Drawn & Quarterly, 2014.

Hernandez, Gilbert. *Chance in Hell.* Seattle: Fantagraphics Books, 2007.

Hernandez, Gilbert. *The Children of Palomar.* Seattle: Fantagraphics Books, 2013.

Hernandez, Gilbert. *Fatima: The Blood Spinners*. Milwaukie, OR: Dark Horse Comics, 2014.

Hernandez, Gilbert. *Heartbreak Soup*. Seattle: Fantagraphics Books, 2007.

Hernandez, Gilbert. *Human Diastrophism*. Seattle: Fantagraphics Books, 2007.

Hernandez, Gilbert. *Julio's Day*. Seattle: Fantagraphics Books, 2013.

Hernandez, Gilbert. "Letters from Venus: Life on Mars." In *Luba and Her Family*, 35–40. Seattle: Fantagraphics Books, 2014.

Hernandez, Gilbert. "Letters from Venus." In *Luba and Her Family*, 21–26. Seattle: Fantagraphics Books, 2014.

Hernandez, Gilbert. "Letters from Venus: Who Cares About Love?" In *Luba and Her Family*, 72–77. Seattle: Fantagraphics Books, 2014.

Hernandez, Gilbert. *Loverboys*. Milwaukie, OR: Dark Horse Comics, 2014.

Hernandez, Gilbert. *Luba and Her Family*. Seattle: Fantagraphics Books, 2014.

Hernandez, Gilbert. *Marble Season*. Montreal: Drawn & Quarterly, 2013.

Hernandez, Gilbert. *Maria M*. Book 1. Seattle: Fantagraphics Books, 2013.

Hernandez, Gilbert. *Ofelia*. Seattle: Fantagraphics Books, 2015.

Hernandez, Gilbert. "Poison River." In *Beyond Palomar*, 7–192. Seattle: Fantagraphics Books, 2007.

Hernandez, Gilbert. *Speak of the Devil*. Milwaukie, OR: Dark Horse Comics, 2008.

Hernandez, Gilbert. *The Troublemakers*. Seattle: Fantagraphics Books, 2009.

Hernandez, Gilbert. "Venus Tells It Like It Is." In *Luba and Her Family*, 222. Seattle: Fantagraphics Books, 2014.

Hernandez, Jaime. "Bay of Threes." In *Penny Century*, 237–49. Seattle: Fantagraphics Books, 2010.

Hernandez, Jaime. *Esperanza*. Seattle: Fantagraphics Books, 2011.

Hernandez, Jaime. *The Girl from H.O.P.P.E.R.S.* Seattle: Fantagraphics Books, 2007.

Hernandez, Jaime. *God and Science: Return of the Ti-Girls*. Seattle: Fantagraphics Books, 2012.

Hernandez, Jaime. "House of Raging Women." In *The Girl from H.O.P.P.E.R.S.*, 26–39. Seattle: Fantagraphics Books, 2007.

Hernandez, Jaime. *The Love Bunglers*. Seattle: Fantagraphics Books, 2014.

Hernandez, Jaime. *Maggie the Mechanic*. Seattle: Fantagraphics Books, 2007.

Hernandez, Jaime. "Maggie vs. Maniakk." In *Maggie the Mechanic*, 90–98. Seattle: Fantagraphics Books, 2007.

Hernandez, Jaime. "Mechanics." In *Maggie the Mechanic*, 30–59. Seattle: Fantagraphics Books, 2007.

Hernandez, Jaime. "Mechan-X." In *Maggie the Mechanic*, 7–14. Seattle: Fantagraphics Books, 2007.

Hernandez, Jaime. *Penny Century*. Seattle: Fantagraphics Books, 2010.

Hernandez, Jaime. "Penny Century, You're Fired!" In *Maggie the Mechanic*, 23. Seattle: Fantagraphics Books, 2007.

Hernandez, Jaime. "Rocky in: Out o' Space." In *Amor y Cohetes*, 106–11. Seattle: Fantagraphics Books, 2008.

Hernandez, Jaime. "Rocky in: Rocket Rhodes." In *Amor y Cohetes*, 187–90. Seattle: Fantagraphics Books, 2008.

Hernandez, Jaime. "Rocky in: Where Are We?" In *Amor y Cohetes*, 147–49. Seattle: Fantagraphics Books, 2008.

Hernandez, Jaime. "Rocky's Birthday Surprise." In *Amor y Cohetes*, 154–67. Seattle: Fantagraphics Books, 2008.

Hernandez, Jaime. "Wigwam Bam." In *Perla La Loca: A Love and Rockets Book*, 6–121. Seattle: Fantagraphics Books, 2007.

Hernandez, Jaime, and Gilbert Hernandez. *Love and Rockets: The Covers*. Seattle: Fantagraphics Books, 2013.

Hernandez, Mario, and Gilbert Hernandez. "Chiro the Indian." In *Love and Rockets: New Stories*. 1: 61–66. Seattle: Fantagraphics Books, 2008.

Hernandez, Jaime, Gilbert Hernandez, and Mario Hernandez. *Love and Rockets: New Stories*. Seattle: Fantagraphics Books, 2008.

Hernandez, Mario. "Intro to Citizen Rex." In *Citizen Rex*, 6. Milwaukie, OR: Dark Horse Comics, 2011.

Hernandez, Mario. *Citizen Rex*. Milwaukie, OR: Dark Horse Comics, 2011.

Hignite, Todd. *The Art of Jaime Hernandez: The Secrets of Life and Death*. New York: Abrams ComicArts, 2010.

Hinds, Harold E., Jr., and Charles M. Tatum. *Not Just for Children: The Mexican Comic Book in the Late 1960s and 1970s*. Westport: Greenwood Press, 1992.

Hirsch, E. D. "In Defense of the Author." In *Intention and Interpretation*, 11–23. Edited by Gary Iseminger. Philadelphia: Temple University Press, 1992.

Hodler, Tim, Dan Nadel, and Frank Santoro. "The Gilbert and Jaime Hernandez Interview." *The Comics Journal* (2012). http://www.tcj.com/the-gilbert-and-jaime-hernandez-interview/.

Hutcheon, Linda. "Historiographic Metafiction: Parody and the Intertextuality of History." In *Intertextuality and Contemporary American Fiction*, 3–32. Edited by P. O'Donnell and Robert Con Davis. Baltimore: Johns Hopkins University Press, 1989.

Hutcheon, Linda. *The Politics of Postmodernism*. London and New York: Routledge, 1989.

Hutcheon, Linda. *A Theory of Adaptation*. London and New York: Routledge, 2006.

Hutcheon, Linda. *A Theory of Parody: The Teachings of Twentieth-Century Art Forms*. New York and London: Methuen, 1985.

Jameson, Fredric. *Postmodernism, or, the Cultural Logic of Late Capitalism*. Durham, NC: Duke University Press, 1991.

Jensen, Jeff. "*Watchmen*: An Oral History." *Entertainment Weekly* (2005). http://www.ew.com/article/2005/10/21/watchmen-oral-history.

Kanellos, Nicolás. "Exiles, Immigrants, and Natives: Hispanic Print Culture in What Became the Mainland of the United States." In *A History of the Book in America, Volume 4: Print in Motion: The Expansion of Publishing and Reading in the United States, 1880–1940*, 312–38. Edited by Carl F. Kaestle and Janice A. Radway. Chapel Hill: University of North Carolina Press, 2009.

Kirkman, Robert. *Invincible* series. Berkeley: Image Comics, 2003–2015.

Kristeva, Julia. "The Bounded Text." In *Desire in Language: A Semiotic Approach to Literature and Art*, 36–63. Edited by Leon S. Roudiez. Translated by Thomas Gora, Alice Jardine, and Leon S. Roudiez. New York: Columbia University Press, 1980.

Kristeva, Julia. "Word, Dialogue, and Novel." In *Desire in Language: A Semiotic Approach to Literature and Art*, 64–91. Edited by Leon S. Roudiez. Translated by Thomas Gora, Alice Jardine, and Leon S. Roudiez. New York: Columbia University Press, 1980.

Kunka, Andrew J. "Review of *God and Science: Return of the Ti-Girls*." *ImageTexT: Interdisciplinary Comics Studies* 7.1 (2013). http://www.english.ufl.edu/imagetext/archives/v7_1/kunka/.

Kurtzman, Harvey, and Wally Wood. "Superduperman." *Mad Archives*. 1: 117–24. New York: DC Comics, 2002.

Lattin, Vernon E. "Contemporary Chicano Novel, 1959–1979." In *Chicano Literature: A Reference Guide*, 184–97. Edited by Julio A. Martínez and Francisco A. Lomelí. Westport, CT: Greenwood Press, 1985.

Lima, Lázaro. *The Latino Body: Crisis Identities in American Literary and Cultural Memory*. New York: New York University Press, 2007.

Lopez, Marissa K. *Chicano Nations: The Hemispheric Origins of Mexican American Literature*. New York: New York University Press, 2011.

McCloud, Scott. *Understanding Comics: The Invisible Art*. New York: Harper Perennial, 1994.

Merino, Ana. "The Bros Hernandez: A Latin Presence in Alternative U.S. Comics." In *Redrawing the Nation: National Identity in Latin/o American Comics*.

Edited by Hector Fernández L'Hoeste and Juan Poblete. New York: Palgrave Macmillan, 2009.

Millán, Elizabeth, and Ernesto Rosen Velásquez. "Latino/a Identity and the Search for Unity: Alcoff, Corlett, and Gracia." In *Forging People: Race, Ethnicity, and Nationality in Hispanic American/Latino/a Thought*, 271–302. Edited by Jorge J. E. Gracia. Notre Dame, IN: University of Notre Dame Press. 2011.

Millar, Mark. *Red Son*. New York: DC, 2014.

Miller, Nancy K. *Subject to Change: Reading Feminist Writing*. New York: Columbia University Press, 1988.

Moore, Alan. *Promethea*. New York: DC, 1999–2005.

Moore, Alan. *Watchmen*. New York: DC, 2014.

Neill, F. Vance. "Gilbert Hernandez as a Rhetor." *ImageTexT: Interdisciplinary Comics Studies* 7.1 (2013). http://www.english.ufl.edu/imagetext/archives/v7_1/neill/.

Nyberg, Amy Kiste. *Seal of Approval*: *The History of the Comics Code*. Jackson: University of Mississippi Press, 1998.

Olea, Raquel. "Feminism: Modern or Postmodern." In *The Postmodernism Debate in Latin America*, 192–200. Edited by John Beverley, Michael Aronna, and José Oviedo. Durham, NC, and London: Duke University Press, 1995.

Oroz, Silvia. *Melodrama: El cine de lágrimas de América latina*. Mexico City: National Autonomous University of Mexico (UNAM), 1995.

Ortego y Gasca, Felipe D. "Chicano Literature from 1942 to the Present." In *Chicano Literature: A Reference Guide*, 137–47. Edited by Julio A. Martínez and Francisco A. Lomelí. Westport, CT: Greenwood Press, 1985.

Padilla, Felix. *Latino Ethnic Consciousness: The Case of Mexican Americans and Puerto Ricans in Chicago*. Notre Dame, IN: University of Notre Dame Press, 1985.

Parker Royal, Derek. "Hernandez Brothers' *Love and Rockets*." In *Critical Survey of Graphic Novels; Heroes and Superheroes*, 517–24. Edited by Bart Beaty and Stephen Weiner. Ipswich, Mass: Salem Press, 2012.

Parker Royal, Derek. "Palomar and Beyond: An Interview with Gilbert Hernandez." *MELUS* 32.3 (2007): 221–46.

Parker Royal, Derek. "The Worlds of the Hernandez Brothers." *ImageTexT: Interdisciplinary Comics Studies* 7.1 (2013). http://www.english.ufl.edu/imagetext/archives/v7_1/introduction/introduction.shtml.

Parker Royal, Derek, and Christopher González, eds. "The Worlds of the Hernandez Brothers." Special issue, *ImageTexT: Interdisciplinary Comic Studies* 1 (Summer 2013). http://www.english.ufl.edu/imagetext/archives/v7_1/.

Pérez-Torres, Rafael. *Mestizaje: Critical Uses of Race in Chicano Culture*. Minneapolis and London: University of Minnesota Press, 2006.

Petersen, Robert. *Comics, Manga, and Graphic Novels: A History of Graphic Narratives*. Santa Barbara, CA: Praeger, 2010.

Pizzino, Christopher. "Autoclastic Icons: Bloodletting and Burning in Gilbert Hernandez's Palomar." *ImageTexT: Interdisciplinary Comics Studies* 7. http://www.english.ufl.edu/imagetext/archives/v7_1/pizzino/.

Potter, Greg. "Kurtzman's Last Solo EC War Story Examined." In *Harvey Kurtzman: Interviews with the Pioneering Cartoonist—The Comics Journal Library*, 134–39. Edited by Denis Kitchen and Paul Buhle. Seattle: Fantagraphics Books, 2006.

Pustz, Matthew. *Comic Book Culture: Fanboys and True Believers*. Jackson: University of Mississippi Press, 1999.

Rius. *Mis supermachos*. [Originally printed as *Los supermachos*] Vol. 3. Mexico: Random House Mondadori, 2010.

Rohrieltner, Marion. "Pan-Latinidad." *Oxford Bibliographies* (2013). doi: 10.1093/OBO/9780199913701-0064.

Rubenstein, Anne. *Bad Language, Naked Ladies, and Other Threats to the Nation: A Political History of Comic Books in Mexico*. Durham, NC, and London: Duke University Press, 1998.

Sabin, Roger. *Comics, Comix and Graphic Novels: A History of Comic Art*. New York and London: Phaidon Press, 1996.

Said, Edward. *Orientalism*. New York: Pantheon Books, 1978.

Saldívar, Ramón. *Chicano Narrative: The Dialectics of Difference*. Madison: The University of Wisconsin Press, 1990.

Saldívar-Hull, Sonia. *Feminism on the Border: Chicana Gender Politics and Literature*. Berkeley: University of California Press, 2000.

Sanders, Julie. *Adaptation and Appropriation*. New York: Routledge, 2006.

Sandoval, Chela. *Methodology of the Oppressed*. Minneapolis: University of Minnesota Press, 2000.

Saxey, Esther. "Desire without Closure in Jaime Hernandez' Love and Rockets." *ImageTexT: Interdisciplinary Comics Studies* 3.1 (2006). http://www.english.ufl.edu/imagetext/archives/v3_1/saxey/.

Schou, Solvej. "'Love and Rockets' Co-Creator Jaime Hernandez on the Comic's 30th Anniversary." *Entertainment Weekly* (2013). http://www.ew.com/article/2013/01/08/capetown-love-and-rockets-anniversary-jaime-hernandez.

Scott, Daerick. "Love, Rockets, Race & Sex." *The Americas Review: A Review of Hispanic Literature and Art of the USA* 23.3–4 (Fall-Winter 1995): 73–106.

Silverblatt, Michael. "Jaime Hernandez and Junot Diaz: *This Is How You Lose Her.*" *Bookworm* (podcast), February 13, 2014. http://www.podcasts.com /kcrws-bookworm/episode/jaime-hernandez-and-junot-diaz-this-is-how-you -lose-her.

Sobel, Marc. "Marc Sobel and Gary Groth." In *The Love and Rockets Companion*, 160–77. Edited by Marc Sobel and Kristy Valenti. Seattle: Fantagraphics Books, 2013.

Sobel, Marc. "Marc Sobel and The Brothers." In *The Love and Rockets Companion*, 120–59. Edited by Marc Sobel and Kristy Valenti. Seattle: Fantagraphics Books, 2013.

Sobel, Marc, and Kristy Valenti, eds. *The Love and Rockets Companion.* Seattle: Fantagraphics Books, 2013.

Stam, Robert. *Literature and Film: A Guide to the Theory and Practice of Film Adaptation.* Hoboken, NJ: Wiley-Blackwell, 2004.

Sullivan, Darcy. "At the Drawing Board with Gilbert." In *Ten Years of Love and Rockets: 1982–1992.* Seattle: Fantagraphics Books, 1992.

Torres-Saillant, Silvio. "Epilogue: Problematic Paradigms: Racial Diversity and Corporate Identity in the Latino Community." In *Latinos: Remaking America*, 435–56. Edited by Marcelo M. Suárez-Orozco and Mariela M. Páez. Berkeley: University of California Press, 2002.

Vargas Dulché, Yolanda. *María Isabel.* Vols. 1–8. Mexico: Mundo Vid, 2005.

Vargas Dulché, Yolanda. *Memín Pinguín.* Vols. 1–28. Mexico: Mundo Vid, 2006–2010.

Vargas, Gabriel. *La familia Burrón.* Vols. 1–14. Mexico: Porrúa, 2010–2016.

Venegas, Daniel. *Las Aventuras De Don Chipote, O Cuando Los Pericos Mamen.* Houston, TX: Arte Público Press, 1998.

Waid, Mark. *Irredeemable.* Los Angeles: Boom, 2009–2012.

Wright, Bradford. *Comic Book Nation: The Transformation of Youth Culture in America.* Baltimore: Johns Hopkins University Press, 2001.

index

ers' lack of knowledge of, 120, 138n43;
self-censoring of, 9–11
comic book stores, 19; alternative sources
and, 119–20; choosing by Comics Code
Authority approval, 9–11; under direct
marketing, 14–15; effects of physical
space in, 9, 118–19; placement of items
in, 61, 119, 121; selection in, 13–15,
119
comic genres, 7; Jaime shifting among, 23,
107, *108*, 111; Los Bros manipulating,
6, 70; parodies of, 50, 105; pastiches
of, 42, 44, *48*, 49; transgressions of,
33, 36, 69
comic influences, on Los Bros, 5, 34, 41,
78, 80; Crumb, 6, 28; Kurtzman, 6, 28,
34–39; Mexican comics, 124–25
comics: analysis rarely taught, 27, 32;
blamed for illiteracy, 9, 136n7; complexity of Latino, 104
Comics Code Authority, 137n14; creation
of, 9–10, 119, 136n11; effects of, 6,
9–10; influence of, 12, 120
The Comics Journal, 141n17; by Fantagraphics Books, 17, 34; Gilbert's
interview for, 83, 139n52, 144n76
coming of age stories, 66, 69–70, 106–7
comix movement, 12–13, 93, 119, 138n28;
Crumb as figurehead of, 35, 39–40;
influence on Los Bros, 17, 34
comiXology (Fantagraphics' digital venue),
19
"Coon Imagery in Will Eisner's *The Spirit*
and Yoland Vargas Dulché's *Memín
Pinguín*" (García), 99–100
copyright, 35, 40–41, 52
creator ownership, 13, 17
Criterion, Jaime's illustrations for, 24

Crumb, Robert: depictions of women, 35,
141n20; as figurehead of comix movement, 12, 35, 39–40; influence on Los
Bros, 6, 23, 28, 34, 134

D'Angelo, Frank, 29, 35, 43
Daredevil, 52
Dark Horse, 22
DC Comics, 22, 38, 52–53, 120, 133
"The Death of the Author" (Barthes), 29
DeCarlo, Dan, 23, 41
Demmers, Jolle, 149n51
demographics, of comic readers, 2, 15, 87
Dennis the Menace, 80
dialogism, 31, 41, 51, 77, 88, 107
Díaz, Junot: Jaime's illustrations for, 24,
74–75; Los Bros' influence on, 136n5,
146n14; praise for Los Bros, 3–4, 75
dictatorships, not featured in *Palomar* saga,
81
digital distribution, 19, 121–22
direct marketing, 13–15, 61, 120–21,
138n32
Disney, suing Air Pirates, 40
distribution system, comic, 15–16
Ditko, Steve, 23
Don Quixote, 42
Drawn & Quarterly, 26

EC comics, 10, 36–37, 41
Esperanza, in *Locas* saga, 23
Espinosa, Frank, 3
ethnic identity, 147n22, 148n40; Chicano,
76–77; Latino, 6, 70–73; of Los Bros'
characters, 69–70, *74,* 77–78
"Exiles, Immigrants, and Natives" (Kanellos), 83–84

Fantagraphics Books, 5, 19; *The Comics Journal* distributed by, 17, 34; Los Bros publishing with, 2, 17–18; *The Sincerest Form of Parody* by, 38–39
Fawcett, 38
feminism, 152n110
Foster, David, 91
Foucault, Michel, 29, 31, 140n12
Fox, Vicente, 125
Fritz, in *Palomar* saga, 22, 69, 102–6, 129
Fritz the Cat (Crumb), 40
From Mafalda to the Supermachos (Foster), 91
Frontera/Borderlands (Anzaldúa), 79
Fumble, in "Rocky" stories, 66

Gabriel y Gabriela (Vargas Dulché), 86
Gaiman, Neil, 3–4, 117, 150n62
gender, 4, 24; comics' male bias, 17, 56, 87; Crumb's depictions of women, 35, 141n20; deconstruction of, 79, 104, 128; idealized masculinity debunked, 50, 55, 56; Los Bros' strong female characters, 17, 59, 80, 92–93, 109, 128; parodies of overly masculine heroes, 44, 106
genres. *See* comic genres
"The Ghoul Man," 126
The Girl from H.O.P.P.E.R.S. (Jaime), 23
Glaser, Jennifer, 82, 89, 146n14, 148n40
Gloria, in *Palomar,* 97, 98
God and Science: The Return of the Ti-Girls (Jaime), 23, 58, 111
González, Christopher, 5, 74–75, 117
González, Juan, 75
Gracia, Jorge J. E., 70, 72, 145n2
graphic novels, 22, 24, 102–5
Gray, Harold, 39
Grip, 22, 118–19

Groth, Gary, 35, 83, 117, 121
Gutíerrez, Antonio, 90–91

Habell-Pallán, 78, 106–7
Hatfield, Charles, 13–14, 32, 150n67; on alternative comics, 4, 138n32; on influences on Los Bros, 17, 34; on *Palomar,* 90, 93, 97; on Pedro Pacotilla, 33–34
Hau, Caroline, 151n81
Heartbreak Soup, 20
"Heartbreak Soup," 83–84
hegemony, subversion of, 3
Help!, 39
Hermerén, Goran, 38
Hernandez, Aurora (mother), love of comic books, 12, 125, 137n24
Hernandez, Gilbert, 47, 80, 113, 146n14; art of, 22–23, 66, 92, 150n67; *Citizen Rex* by, 4, 66–67; comic industry and, 15–16, 22, 35; critique of *Poison River* plot, 130–31; Crumb and, 35, 134, 141n20; intertextuality of, 23, 30; interviews with, 24, 82–83, 138n46, 139n47, 139n52, 144n76; *Love and Rockets* and, 17, 138n46; *Luba* and *Luba's Comics and Stories* by, 18–19; not reading Mexican comics, 93–94, 100; parody of Memín Pinguín, 33–34; politics and, 7, 77, 147n26; writing process of, 25–26, 45–46, 80, 84–85, 101. See also *Love and Rockets; Palomar* saga
Hernandez, Jaime, 19, 35, 66, 100; art of, 5, 22–24, 133, 136n6; illustrating for Díaz, 4, 24; influences on, 41, 105; interviews with, 74–75, 106; on Latino identities, 74–75; Maggie and, 114, 143n72; narrative style of, 107, 109, 112, 132–33; superhero genre and, 57,

as comic book reader, 62–64; disappointment in superheroes, *55*, 56; Jaime and, 114, 143n72; lack of involvement in politics, 7, 109–11; Latino culture and, 7, 50–51; Latino identity of, 69–70, 72–73, *74*; Penny Century and, 112, 152n100; Rena Titañón and, 7, 112; in "The Return of the Ti-Girls," *60*, 61–63; sexuality of, 106–7; in varying genres, 105–6, *108*, 111; in Zimbodia, 109–10

Maggie the Mechanic, in *Locas* saga, 23, *48*

Manuel, in *Palomar,* 94

Marble Season (Gilbert), 24–26

María Isabel (Vargas Dulché), 79–80, 91, 150n63; *Palomar* compared to, 86–90, 93–94; race in, 88–89, 149n61, 150n62

Maria M (Gilbert), 22, 24, 102–3

marketing, 18–19, 72, 138n28. *See also* direct marketing

marketplace, 6, 8, 9–11, 13. *See also* comic book stores

Marvel, 41, 53, 120, 133

Marvel Universe, 123

Marxism, 76–77, 136n8

mass culture, 9, 12, 102, 137n15. *See also* pop culture

McCloud, Scott, 32

"Mechan-X" (Jaime), 6, 50, 79; as pastiche of genres, 42, 44, 49

melodrama, 61, 105–6

Melodrama (Oroz), 85

Memín Pinguín (Vargas Dulché and Valencia), 33–34, 99–100, 124–25

Merino, Ana, 77

mestizaje. See racial hybridity

Mestizaje (Perez Torres), 89

Methodology of the Oppressed (Sandoval), 104–5

Mexico, 89; comic industry in, 10–11, 87, 137n18; comics from, 79–80, 86–88, 93–94, 100, 115, 124–25; debate about *Memín Pinguín* in, 33, 99–100; in Los Bros' heritage, 82, 112–13; nationalism of, 90–92, 99–100

Millar, Mark, 52

Miller, Frank, 52

Miller, Nancy K., 30

modernism, 151n80

monster, in "BEM," *45,* 45–48

Moore, Alan, 3, 4, 38, 52–53, 136n6

Morales, Gil, 2

motherhood, 60, 111

movies, 86, 90; Fritz's, 69, 106; in *Palomar,* 102–5, 132

music, punk, 17

Nadel, Dan, 139n52, 144n76

narratives, 32, *51;* characters taking control of, 103, 132; Latino *vs.* Anglophone, 103–4, 113; Los Bros,' 17, 41, 42, 77

narrative techniques, 5–6; Gilbert's, 45–46; Jaime's, 109, 112

nationalism: long-distance, 149n50, 149n51; Mexican, 90–92, 99–100

Neill, F. Vance, 103

New Tales of Old Palomar (Children of Palomar), 106

New York City, 13, 73–74

New Yorker, 24

New York Times, Locas strip printed in, 23, 111

nostalgia, 80, 82

Not Just for Children: The Mexican Comic Book in the Late 1960s and 1970s (Hinds and Tatum), 87

Nyberg, Amy Kiste, 9–10, 136n11